Book Reviews

I have been in the field of Early Childhood Education for 36 years, and this book brought back so many tender memories. As a former Preschool teacher, I can remember feeling overwhelmed at times and yet also so thankful for the opportunity to help impact the projected path for our youngest learners. Darlene Northam has authored an inspiring book to help remind Early Childhood Educators of the tremendous role they play in helping mold the lives of every child they have the privilege to embrace if you need a reminder of your "Why," – this book is a MUST READ!

G. Lee Taylor
Head Start Early Childhood Education Director

Educators, notwithstanding their length of time in the pedagogical field, would benefit from reading You Are Not Just A Teacher; You Are So Much More! In this book, Darlene Northam rescues us from abandoning or abusing our calling, reminds us of our why, and realigns our focus, all while using our physical attributes, personal testimonies, divine insights, biblical scriptures, and powerful prayers as sources for introspection and transformation. The words penned in this piece will no doubt become as classic and timeless as the highly popular 1997 book by Harry K. Wong. Therefore, it is immensely advantageous for school divisions, educational organizations, educators, and even parents to use this book as a means of professional investment and understanding. This book is an invaluable resource!

Dr. Angerina L. Jones, *D.M., Ed.D.*
Assistant Principal

Wow! What a transformational read! This body of work is riddled with nuggets that anyone in any field of "heart" care as a profession can benefit from. The author's uncanny ability to draw the reader in while challenging yet encouraging the reader to always strive for better is a daunting yet accomplished task. I walked away from the journey feeling inspired, encouraged, and, yes, even convicted. This resource pushes one to take a good look at themselves and encourages one to be the change agent one heart at a time!

Marcus M. Northam, *B.A. Psy., M.A. Practical Theology*

"You Are Not Just A Teacher; You Are So Much More!" is engaging, warm, and deeply personal. Darlene Northam's genuine passion for education shines through each page, resonating with educators on a profound level. This book is an exceptional resource that celebrates the transformative role of educators in shaping the lives of their students. It encourages educators to embrace their unique ability to touch hearts and minds and serves as a reminder that education is not just about imparting knowledge but about building lasting connections, leaving a positive legacy, and making a difference that can never be erased.

Lynnetta M. Seabury, *BSBM, MM*
Founder/CEO BridgeWay Preparatory Christian School

Throughout the reading, I was consistently engaged and excited to read what was to come! You were clear, relatable, and so transparent. Each of your life and classroom stories brought a strong sense of the value of not only who you are but who you are as an educator leading to help others. I am proud, excited, and honored to have been chosen to read and give feedback.

Brandi R. Roberts, *M.S., L.P.S.C.*

You Are Not Just A Teacher; You Are So Much More! Cultivating the Heart of Educators
Copyright © 2023 Darlene Northam
www.darlenenortham.com

Published by Spirit Filled Creations LLC
www.SpiritFilledCreations.com
Email: SpiritFilledCreations7@gmail.com

This book or parts thereof may not be reproduced in any form, stored in a retrieval system, or transmitted in any form by any means – electronic, mechanical, photocopy, recording, or otherwise – without prior written permission of the publisher and authors, except as provided by United States of America copyright law.

All rights reserved.
Scriptures marked NIV are taken from the NEW INTERNATIONAL VERSION (NIV): Scripture taken from THE HOLY BIBLE, NEW INTERNATIONAL VERSION ®. Copyright© 1973, 1978, 1984, 2011 by Biblica, Inc.TM. Used by permission of Zondervan. Scriptures marked AMP are taken from the AMPLIFIED BIBLE (AMP): Scripture taken from the AMPLIFIED® BIBLE, Copyright © 1954, 1958, 1962, 1964, 1965, 1987 by the Lockman Foundation Used by Permission. (www.Lockman.org). Scriptures marked NLT are taken from the HOLY BIBLE, NEW LIVING TRANSLATION (NLT): Scriptures taken from the HOLY BIBLE, NEW LIVING TRANSLATION, Copyright© 1996, 2004, 2007 by Tyndale House Foundation. Used by permission of Tyndale House Publishers, Inc., Carol Stream, Illinois 60188. All rights reserved. Used by permission. Scripture quotations marked TPT are from The Passion Translation®. Copyright © 2017, 2018, 2020 by Passion & Fire Ministries, Inc. Used by permission. All rights reserved. ThePassionTranslation.com. Scriptures marked ESV are taken from THE HOLY BIBLE, ENGLISH STANDARD VERSION (ESV): Scriptures taken from THE HOLY BIBLE, ENGLISH STANDARD VERSION ® Copyright© 2001 by Crossway, a publishing ministry of Good News Publishers. Used by permission.
Cover Design: Darlene Northam, Spirit Filled Creations

International Standard Book Number: 978-1-7342948-6-6

First Edition

Printed in the United States of America

Dedication

*To the educator who needs a reminder
of how influential and essential you are;
I love you to life.*

Thank You

Mount Lebanon Christian Academy, where I began my journey and call as an out-of-the-box educator and a foundation builder for young children.

Suffolk Head Start is where I became astutely aware of my inner strength and vulnerability. Because of you, I acquired the push to become the phenomenal educator I am today.

And lastly, to BridgeWay Preparatory Christian School, thank you for my first platform to present at a teacher's retreat. Your invite was the open door for what was to come.

Samuel Jones, *Sam with the Cam*, thank you for the amazing photos.

Only God gets the Glory, The Honor, and The Praise!

Acknowledgments

To God be All the glory, honor, and praise for this accomplishment.

I wish to thank my exceptional husband, Pastor Marcus M. Northam, for the rock and avid supporter he is. To my children, Goldie, Alicia, Nicki, Mike, Denna, and Markell, thank you for every word of encouragement that cheered me on to the finish line.

Shevea Hayes and Shannon Etheridge, who, without hesitation, celebrated and encouraged me when I first told them I would write a book. To my Bestie, Coach Tahisha P. Thompson, for believing I can do anything I put my mind to. To my prereaders, Pastor Marcus M. Northam, Dr. Angerina Jones, Lynetta Seabury, Brandi Roberts, and G. Lee Taylor, you guys are amazing.

Thank you to my family, friends, and loved ones who continued to inspire and pray for me.

And lastly, to my dear friend, Bestie, book coach, and publisher, Monique Jewell Anderson, the real GOAT, you are a phenomenal woman. Thank you for your hard work and dedication and seeing this assignment come to fruition.

Table of Contents

From The Educator Midwife	9
Introduction	11
THE HEART OF A TEACHER	15
THE MOUTH OF A TEACHER	41
THE EYES OF A TEACHER	61
THE EARS OF A TEACHER	81
THE HANDS OF A TEACHER	97
THE ARMS OF A TEACHER	113
THE FINAL WORDS FOR TEACHERS	117
About The Author	119

From The Educator Midwife

Dear Educator, this amazing resource has a singular goal: to touch your heart.

This book endeavors to speak to the dynamic state of who you are while encouraging you to address the needs of your students that are not scholastic in nature.

As a mom and educator, I firmly believe children must be taught with the whole child in mind. Academic content is vital in the learning process; however, there is more to educating than relating information in a stack of outdated books. I think authentic instruction occurs when we allow ourselves to go further than traditional means have permitted.

You Are Not Just A Teacher; You Are So Much More! shares my passion as an educator by highlighting insightful nuggets concerning challenges faced in our field of education. There are many needs that are significant, which is why many of our students have gotten lost in the cracks. With this in mind, this book tests the thought process of employing essential parts of our anatomy in a learning environment. In addition, I share my philosophy of why it is necessary to relinquish traditional practices and status quo teaching to become more intentional.

You Are Not Just A Teacher; You Are So Much More!
Darlene Northam

Seeing yourself as a legacy builder will give you the fortitude to leave a mark on students' lives that can never be erased.

Darlene Northam
Pre-Elementary ED., M.A.

Introduction

The Covid19 pandemic drastically shifted life's norms as we knew it. With every part of the globe affected, change was imminent, and its reach altered everything. Automotive dealerships, restaurants, banks, healthcare, department stores, and churches of all denominations had to become innovative to remain relevant. The most affected, I believe, were our schools and educational system. With the world at a standstill, what would our students do when the buildings they spent most of their days in were closed? What strategies were in place to continue their educational pursuits? What things were expendable, and who decided what remained? No matter how much life was altered, one thing would stay constant: the need for teachers.

Someone had to communicate with parents and guardians, provide guidance and instruction, administer exams, and care for the students. At the end of the day, there is no substitute for a warm embrace, a high-five, a great job, thanks for trying, or a genuine concern of a teacher. Unfortunately, no matter how much the educational system continues to evolve, I am afraid great educators will become a rare commodity. Many have become cold and desensitized and have forgotten the impact of a smile on the right student. It can be life-altering to take a moment to listen to a hurting or disappointed student. The truth is that these students thrive and become more confident when educators go beyond the status quo and teach more than academics. Sometimes, to reach and teach one, an empathic ear and a sympathetic heart are required to aid struggling students who fight every day just to get up and come to school, let alone do well.

You Are Not Just A Teacher; You Are So Much More! was written to touch the hearts of educators and teachers, those called to mold, model, and change the lives of our youth by engaging essential parts of our anatomy used in the learning process. This book endeavors to speak to the core of whom teachers are while encouraging this same population to be sensitive and proactive when interacting with students. I believe it is our emotional center that dictates our encounters. In other words, the condition of our hearts will determine how we speak, see, hear, and touch our students.

I am you. I am an educator and teaching professional with twenty-two-plus years of experience in and out of the classroom. I love children and have embraced the chance to work with them since my early thirties. However, I did not see myself paving the way for so many youths. However, after realizing this would be a life-long journey, I knew I needed to continue learning. My formal education allowed me to obtain two associate degrees: Early Childhood Education and General Studies. In addition, I have a Bachelor's in Interdisciplinary Studies. And lastly, I earned a Master's in Pre-Elementary education. As such, I have learned much through mistakes, frustration, disappointments, and life experiences. I firmly believe that teaching should foster a love for learning, so much so, that if a student wanted to reach for the stars, there would be no doubt that he could. It's my goal to get us to a place where we see ourselves as legacy builders.

I desire that You Are Not Just A Teacher; You Are So Much More! will remind teachers who may have forgotten their why a reason to fully reengage in the learning process. Academics will always be an essential focal point of learning; however, many students will only absorb educational content once emotional barriers are broken. The conversion will occur once students know they matter and are partners with us on this journey. I hope to highlight simplistic teaching methods as I share my experiences to build and foster relationships you can use with your students. As I provide insight into the educational process without relying solely on books, we will focus on becoming a part of their world and meeting them where they are. Hence, the best way to break through emotional, social, physical, mental, or educational barriers is by allowing yourself to become more intentional and sensitive to more than the student's instructional needs.

I

The Heart of a Teacher

"Among the things you can give and still keep are your word, a smile, and a grateful heart."
Zig Ziglar

I accepted a private school principal position, which was more than I had bargained for. However, it was a great lesson because it taught me that just because I could do something doesn't equate to what I should do. And because I made some not-so-sound decisions, I was forced to split my days and work in the office and the classroom. Consequently, I was emotionally and mentally taxed and could not keep up with the pace. Moreover, the school year was ending, and I needed a week to regroup. Well, during my end-of-the-year evaluation, I was informed my contract as principal would not be renewed. The nerve, I thought, why should I even care? I was burnt out anyway. With resentment and disappointment at the core of my decision process, I vowed never to step foot in another classroom. I couldn't take another disrespectful parent, unrealistic goals, unruly kids, etc. So, I decided this was it for me. I declared I was done with teaching and wanted no part of the classroom again, and I walked away.

Abandoning one of the most fulfilling things in my life was difficult. At this juncture, I couldn't imagine doing anything else, especially since I had been an educator for most of my adulthood. Teaching was more than a position or career choice; it was who I was. No matter where or whom I was with, I always found a way to make it a teachable moment. Learning was more than standing in front of a classroom day after day telling students what to do and how they should be doing it; it was the experience – and it all derived from what I call a matter of the heart. Let me explain.

I believe who we are and what we do as educators stem from the condition of the heart. In other words, the matter of the heart is the total of the content that lies deep within us. Our emotions, thoughts, and will are all part of our makeup. These things affect how we encounter our students. If our heart is not in a good place on any given day, it will hinder positive interactions with our students. When our hearts are hurting or bruised by others, we tend to be more careless with handling those we are responsible for. Therefore, we must take the proper steps to nurture our hearts with things that produce flourishing outcomes. Listen, the heart of an emotionally unstable teacher will result in exchanges that affect how she speaks and respond to students. More importantly, this will undoubtedly determine how they are taught. So, I reiterate teaching is a matter of our hearts, and with every passing second, minute, and hour of the day, we are on display. What we model before our students speaks volumes of who we are. Walk with me as I share the various phases of the heart.

Let's consider the physical heart. The heart is located in the center of the chest cavity. It is the most important organ within the framework of the human body. Though a small muscle, it is powerful enough to pump blood throughout the body, ensuring it gets to every organ, cell, nerve, and tissue. This vital organ forcibly and consistently provides ample blood supply to sustain life to accomplish this incredible task. In fact, without the heart's capacity to do so, the body loses its vitality to thrive and function effectively. When this happens, every part of the body suffers. For example, if blood (containing oxygen) rich nutrients don't get to the brain, the body becomes lifeless.

Teachers, we cannot take our hearts' health for granted. We should try to create a better balance for the stresses met. It is also essential to decompress when we feel overwhelmed by the tasks of being an educator. Occasionally, we will have disruptive students who throw our whole circle time routine out of sync. More times than not, this can create anxiety because we want our days to flow smoothly. However, experiencing more than expected stress could affect your heart adversely. Placing too much strain beyond its ability to operate optimally is not wise because physical and emotional stressors can damage it. Both can cause irreversible harm, potentially leading to health problems or more serious matters like death.

In a day and time when education dynamics have changed drastically due to Covid19 and the like, educators at all levels must figure out how to balance life and the classroom. For example, teachers coming from college have no experience or reference point for teaching virtually. I am sure their student teaching was done in a traditional classroom, as was mine. What about the seasoned teachers who had to learn to navigate new technology connected to online learning? This could potentially incite several types of emotions. You are responsible for students in the building and those in a virtual setting. The traditional school life as you once knew it had been altered forever. Many teachers lack the fortitude to work until retirement due to insensitive and demanding work environments. An online article stated that the pandemic had prompted more teachers to consider early retirement or a new career. A survey revealed that during Covid-19, many educators were undecided about whether they would work until retirement. However, in "March 2020, 74% of teachers said they expected to work until retirement. A year later, that figure dropped to 69%. Undoubtedly, some educators were unsure about staying or leaving the profession altogether. That number rose from "16% to 22%."

These and many other factors have compounded the stress level on the heart of those who care for students. My friends have shared a decline in their mental and emotional health since the pandemic. For example, one of my closest girlfriends would break out in hives when she became too anxious concerning the ongoing changes in instruction implementation. Another friend had heart palpitations for the same reason. She tried to ignore it for a while, but the condition escalated; therefore, her doctor placed her on temporary medicine for depression. Other associates chose to self-medicate as well as indulge in other unhealthy activities. In addition, they have expressed a need to seek professional help along with taking something to aid with sleeping. On a more transparent note, I have a very close relative who has been in the field for twenty-five years and, as recently as May '21, had a stent placed in her heart because of the increased strain brought on by the demands of her job. In her transparency, she shared with me that she got to work at 7:00 a.m., stayed most evenings until 7:00 or 8:00 p.m., and still took work home. Amidst all this, she taught in a dual-learning environment where she did not have adequate help to assist the overwhelming numbers in the classroom. For those experiencing some of the same, this tension cannot be suitable for the organ as it is not built to withstand the longevity and weight of such burdens.

Though some statistics show the overwhelming burden placed on our teachers, I am unsure if anyone has solved the problem. Now, I realize other occupations are taxing; however, the rapid spread of the pandemic placed those working in educational institutions to the point of breaking.

Hence, in a recent online study published on November 28, 2022, entitled "Teachers felt more Covid anxiety than healthcare workers"; the results were saddening. I quote, "By far, teachers had the highest odds of reporting anxiety – 40% higher than healthcare workers." Compared to office workers, teachers ranked "20% higher and 30% higher than a member of other categories." I can only imagine responding to preschoolers learning new protocols and juggling online and in-person pupils. I am sure the magnitude of anxiety was experienced differently, predicated on the instructor's gender and grade level taught. I say this because women tend to respond differently to stress than men, and it doesn't show up the same in their bodies.

Working with K-4 students with an average classroom size of seventeen little ones for twenty-plus years was draining. There were days and sometimes weeks when it seemed nothing had happened as planned. My anxiety was elevated on those days, and I needed a massage. My therapist suggested I increase their frequency because of the number of trigger points I carried in my back, neck, and shoulders. Getting them at least twice a month relaxed me and created a space for emotional balance.

To cope with the frustration that comes with the job, it is necessary to reset. What I mean by this is to stop, evaluate, and do a body check. Sometimes, we may need to sit at our desks while the students work independently and take deep, slow breaths through our mouths and out through our noses.

I have found this to be a great stress reliever, taking the pressure off our hearts. Moreover, it will relax our muscles because we tend to tense up when worried. I am not trying to sound morbid; however, people can live without a kidney or gallbladder, but I don't know anyone surviving without a heart. For this reason, we must take every occasion to ensure that this organ stays healthy and continues to be that life-sustaining force it has been designed to be. Just as attending to our physical heart is essential, it is equally significant to guard our spiritual heart.

SCRIPTURE

The Bible tells us in Proverbs 4:23, above all else, guard your heart, for everything you do flows from it (NIV). This is saying, fellow educators, that we should be cautious and sensitive with what we allow to enter our hearts—things like doubt, insecurities, jealousy, and many other things. The things in our hearts directly impact our choices, which can alter the lives of our students, both negatively and positively. In other words, good will produce good, but the same holds true for bad. The word guard means we are to watch over as a means of protecting and not allowing anything or anyone to bring harm. Therefore, we must place a censor over our hearts, so we don't damage our students with things that come from our mouths. The Bible tells us the heart will say whatever it is full of (Matthew 12:34 NIV). With the climate of this era, gun reform, social injustices, and hate crimes rising, keeping our hearts from evil thoughts hasn't been easy.

I can attest to this. As a result, it becomes necessary to immediately deal with the damaging thoughts that invade our peace, so they don't take root. Choosing not to deal with a destructive mindset can create fertile ground for an irritant to grow. Over time, our hearts can become full of toxins and emotional baggage. The excess can spill over into our conversations and interactions in the classroom. If unchecked, our verbal exchanges would sound like this, "If you sat down when I told you to, you would not have dropped your food. Now, you have nothing to eat, and it's your fault." These words demonstrate no empathy, and it's because our hearts have become cold and desensitized. Therefore, I encourage you to assess your emotions daily. Doing so will assist you in guarding your heart against those critical feelings lurking to take up permanent residence.

Though we fight through our negative emotions most days, we occasionally falter. When we do, we must pull our emotions out of the moment to resolve conflict because the last thing we want is to leave a student wounded by our words or actions. For example, let's take the same scenario as stated above to see how it could have played out differently when the student dropped their food. As a result, the teacher could have reminded him of his decision to ignore her request, thereby placing the responsibility for what happened on him. Doing it this way allows the pupil to reflect on his disobedience and the need to respond appropriately the next time he's asked to sit down. Accordingly, when we view things with a sensitive heart, our words will have a more reassuring outcome.

As those who have been trusted with key positions in the lives of children, we must always be regarded as uncompromising. Don't be misled, nor take for granted that our hearts mirror the core of who we are. Because we are schoolteachers, the condition of our heart will affect every aspect of our engagement with our scholars, beginning with how we see them. If not properly maintained, it will also change how we speak and touch their lives. Moreover, the state of our core will also dictate how we hear and respond to them.

Knowing that our heart's condition will be seen in every aspect of our student interaction, we must consistently evaluate our exchanges to ensure they stay positive. One sure way is to be intentional about what we allow to enter our hearts. Think about it. Our senses are alive and well; whatever they encounter will produce an effect. For instance, if we decide to watch something on television that makes us upset, the likelihood of us expressing how we feel about it will potentially be negative. Unfortunately, we may not recognize how much it has disturbed our peace until there is a trigger. Look at it this way. You and your student are having an innocent conversation when something said triggers a negative response in you. Not making the association until later in the day, it becomes clear that the trigger was related to the T.V. show you watched earlier in the week. Protect your peace by guarding your heart.

Another example of being conscious of what crosses the doorsill of our emotional core is to monitor any degrading conversations we entertain with co-workers. Sometimes, their words penetrate our ears without realizing it and take root in our subconsciousness. Before we know it, we have formed a judgment. Shortly thereafter, we run into that student, and the conversation about him immediately resurfaces. When we open our mouths, we find our words are harsh and uncaring. As a result, he may walk away feeling doleful. Once words have been released, we cannot retract them. It's like taking a nail out of wood – while it has been removed, the hole it created is still there. Children are no different. The heart of a child is impressionable, and whatever we have said or shown them by our actions will be replayed in their minds. We are taught that from birth to five years of age, they are like sponges – they soak up everything. For this reason, we should become more intentional by ensuring we nurture our feelings with pure and honest things. More than anything, our goal is to leave them with positive imprints.

So, protect your heart at all costs. It is valuable; therefore, I encourage you to prioritize self-care as often as possible. Try watching family-oriented movies, taking nature walks, and relaxing. Escape by reading a good book that can take you to places your mind will enjoy exploring. Allow yourself to discover and evolve so that you are transformed into someone greater.

Whatever we don't prevent from crossing the threshold of our mind gets watered by our thoughts and will soon grow into an action. That action will soon become a practice. Whatever becomes a part of our daily routine, good, bad, right, wrong, or indifferent, sets a trajectory for our life in motion. We must become good stewards of our emotions and protect them from anything that can be used to harden them.

It's important to note that a heart conversion will not occur until there is a spiritual one. We have to be willing to open ourselves up to see what we look like on the inside, and I know that can be challenging. More than likely, we won't like what we see. We are not always conscious of the ugliness that comes from within until a situation warrants an observation. According to Psalms 139:23-24 (AMP), David permitted God to search his heart. He tells God to examine him thoroughly so He would know his heart. David tells God to test him as a means of revealing any anxious thoughts and also reveal any wicked or hurtful things. Life has a way of presenting obstacles. When it does, it becomes difficult to hide the destructive behaviors that tend to lurk deep within. Eventually, they leak out into our actions, and others will be affected one way or the other.

Let's Pray:

> *Father, I thank you that my heart is pure and free from judgments and criticism. I pray that any part of my heart damaged by societal influences or anything from my past is*

*being healed and restored so that my words will encourage and
release confidence in my students.
In Jesus' Name, Amen.*

THE WHY

I believe it is imperative for us to keep our why at the forefront of our minds. As we continue this journey, our onward movement will be remembered long after each pupil has graduated and advanced to bigger and better opportunities. In the greater scheme of things, we are at the center of it all, much like the heart that provides life-giving nutrients to each body part. Note that we assume a similar position that sustains each impressionable mind. In other words, we are accountable for the rhythm and flow of our classrooms, which is hinged upon our mood. The year I went to Head Start, I met a four-year-old named Timothy, who changed my life forever. When I met him, he was shy, unkept, and did not want to be in my classroom. However, Timothy thrived over time with patience and a plan for his success. It was because I worked on keeping my heart right. That little boy reminded me of my why. So, I urge you never to forget why you started this journey. What prompted you to believe children needed you or, more importantly, what you had to offer? Think about your original intent for starting this pilgrimage. It may not have been to make it a career, but something happened, and you fell in love with the idea of making a difference in the lives of children just as I did.

*You Are Not Just A Teacher; You Are So Much More!
Darlene Northam*

Nothing is more rewarding than seeing a child struggling from day one morph into an amazing model student. I am not just talking about academically but socially, emotionally, and mentally. You saw their hope and confidence to keep going the day it connected. You were there when his heart began to beat again with excitement because of your unfailing encouragement. It takes a special person to continue giving when it appears nothing is working. But you kept smiling. In addition, you continued to embrace your students when you felt like you had nothing else to give. To your credit, you didn't complain. Celebrate that! What a great spark of emotions you must have felt when you witnessed, for the very first time, your mentee holding his head up to look at your face and speak to you. Remember how instrumental you were with involving the parents in his learning process? This transpired because of your firm stance not to quit but to see it through. Our hearts are designed to operate with a continuous current. Every time it pumps, there should be evidence of love and patience being poured into the atmosphere of our classrooms; the goal is to penetrate the tough layers in their lives. We must grab hold of the things that push us out of our comfort zone and challenge us to improve.

I only improved at becoming a more empathetic teacher because of my willingness to embrace my struggles as a child and not be ashamed of growing up in poverty, much like the students I taught. Then and only then was I able to identify my why as demonstrated within Timothy's battles and respond appropriately to his emotional trauma. His transformation directly correlated with me getting out of the way and allowing my compassion, not my head, to lead me. Otherwise, I would have mishandled him and failed at the opportunity to walk with him through his emotional healing process.

Post Covid19, and now more than ever, it is important to approach each school year with a refreshed heart. Considering each child's uniqueness, begin the year by allowing yourself to be open to new ideas and possibilities. Your flexibility will present unlimited opportunities to engage your students and create a cultivating environment for them to advance. This is what makes you great. You can bring out the best in your pupils. As channels that provide a continuous stream of support, never forget what it felt like to be a kid. Though our experiences vary, they are relevant in helping to meet their needs. How we were cultured as children shape the kind of instructors we become. Unfortunately, not all of our childhood encounters have pleasant memories. Hence, my journey with Timothy warranted my dysfunctional upbringing because it reminded me that something good could come from situations that seem dismal. Just as I had to, stepping back and looking at our heart's content will become imperative. This becomes beneficial in touching the lives of youth in a way they'll strive to become the best version of themselves. In doing so, it will cause you to do the same.

You Are Not Just A Teacher; You Are So Much More!
Darlene Northam

RECALIBRATE

Many of us drive our cars daily, which causes a lot of wear and tear. As a result, some of the electrical and mechanical features can stop working or become faulty. When this happens, we take our cars to a mechanic because we don't want to cause more damage or place ourselves in jeopardy of being liable for an accident. Once in the shop, we discovered our car needed to be recalibrated. Well, our hearts are no different. Due to our fast-paced society, acknowledging our check engine light is on becomes necessary. However, something could be going on that we may be overlooking or have not taken the time to assess.

All hearts need recalibrating. The Cambridge Dictionary defines recalibrate as one's ability to change how you do something or think about a particular thing. When I became more sensitive to the condition of my heart, I altered how I operated. I was more astute in how I constructed and implemented my lessons. I recalibrated by committing to a standard of instruction that allowed my students to be authentically who they were in their learning process. Sometimes, they just wanted to be silly. Hence, they had my permission to do that and not feel condemned for doing so. Let me give you an example. The students were instructed to create a tree with the material they had been given. Instead of interjecting my biases about how the children's tree should look, I changed my perspective. I allowed them to share their creativity no matter how different they were. There were also times when my students took paint meant for canvasses but painted their bodies instead. Their love for exploring is essential in the growing and maturing process and can make a difference in how they learn. Changing my views on how they acquired a particular skill set gave them the confidence to inspire their creative juices. They deserved to walk away with experiences that impacted their hearts, not just what they learned.

We know that a great amount of absorption occurs because of exploration. And as I became more flexible, I fashioned my classroom setting to mirror the material taught. For example, if I were instructing on bugs and butterflies, my room would come alive and resemble their habitat with an assortment of insects and butterflies, colorful nets displayed, and various books on the topic. I purchased plastic replicas of creepy crawlers to reinforce the lesson as I placed them in corners, on shelves, and on the walls. The day's highlight was going outside to catch bugs for our science experiments. You may not be able to duplicate this method with every lesson. Still, I want you to try things that provide variety in the student's engagement and allow for something fresh and new. Sometimes, it's a matter of making small revisions to how you present or execute an idea. Trust me; one modification can mean the difference in how your students grasp a particular concept or skill. This ideology produced a different viewpoint that helped me to be more excited and engaging at my job.

Listen, don't make the mistake of becoming so familiar with your lesson plans that you neglect your responsibility to periodically grade yourselves to see how well you are doing. We want to remain conscious that we should constantly be evolving. Doing so will inspire us to see the need for reevaluating where we are. Not being able to see the need to modify how we do things is one of the reasons why recalibration is necessary.

A great place to begin is by recalibrating our attitudes. First, it is important to note how we respond to our students. This mindset will be reflected in how we show up for work. Everything we do sets the tone for what happens next, which will become evident in our speech and body language. Displaying an uplifting demeanor will send a positive feeling that we care and are committed. Therefore, we must remain consistent in our ability to pump hope into those we encounter. Though strained by challenges, you are still instrumental in providing a nurturing atmosphere. We know the instructional settings are difficult to manage due to the stringent expectations of supervising dual classrooms.

Conversely, no matter how many changes are implemented, you must remain that unique unwavering force. You do this by showing up and making sure that your emotions are in a place of inspiration. Nevertheless, I ask that you be dedicated to demonstrating kindness because you have no idea what your students may be confronted with.

You Are Not Just A Teacher; You Are So Much More!
Darlene Northam

In fact, my decision to adjust how I interacted with my pupils was important because it prompted me to look at how I had become judgmental. Though subtle, I had formed opinions based on their parent's issues. Once I acknowledged this about myself, I became less biased. It didn't happen immediately, but I took the necessary steps to ensure I challenged how I looked at them. Somehow, I had fooled myself into thinking that I was better than my students, and I wasn't. I had struggles and situations just as they did. The only difference was that I stood out front trying to help them navigate life just as someone had once helped me. As I share this, I am reminded of Ms. Thomas. She was responsible for me coming out of my shell. She showed me something I wasn't getting at home, reassurance. I remember the day she placed her arms around my small, timid frame because I was crying. Her soft words of affirmation gave me the confidence to do the math problem, causing my meltdown. She assured me all would be okay because of her commitment to being more than my teacher. My loud outburst became soft whimpers within a few minutes until I stopped crying altogether.

Educators like Ms. Thompson will forever be etched in our memories. The same holds true for the students we have the privilege of influencing. Embracing that you are fulfilling your purpose is rewarding all by itself. Therefore, having the courage to shift your outlook could mean the difference between a student succeeding or failing. Our ability to pivot is a must. It may require a huge adjustment, but it's worth it. No amount of money can satisfy seeing a student barely making it rise to the challenge of finishing second in the class. Subsequently, watching a student who once cried due to the loneliness of not having family support declare that he will succeed no matter what is priceless. Keep your heart positive because perception matters.

As conduits needing recalibrating, we provide optimism by ensuring that we stay in tune with our surroundings to detect when something is wrong. This can be difficult, especially if we don't know our students. Having overcrowded rooms doesn't make it any easier. One way to address this is to learn something unique about each of our scholars so that whenever something seems off, it's a good chance that we are already in tune. By incorporating an awareness of their needs, you will gain trust from them that you didn't have before. Know that it's a process, so take it one day at a time and celebrate your accomplishments. Don't be too hard on yourself by harping on what you didn't get right because, prayerfully, you will have another day to try again. Use those mishaps as training. Staying hopeful was a great way to keep my head on straight and not allow frustration to get me down. There were days when talking to myself kept me sane. Possibilities are endless when we learn to look on the bright side. As intricate role models, we must say yes even when our minds say no to going the extra mile. ***Our charge is to continue giving when we don't feel like it.*** For my student,

Timothy, to thrive and overcome the obstacles surrounding his emotional barriers, I decided to become vulnerable. As uncomfortable as it may have been initially, I could not allow my old way of viewing things to hamper my need for greater responsibility.

We should commit to doing heart checks by asking ourselves questions that cause us to be introspective. Did I allow someone or something to upset me today? Was I kind despite what was said or done? Why did I become frustrated by my student's response? When we are honest with the necessary examinations, we will become more sensitive to the external and internal forces that serve as triggers. Consistency is the steadying energy that holds everything together. Because we shape young minds and promote the confidence that is hidden by shame and guilt, it is essential for us to speak words that incite promise. Where there is a lack of family support, we offer a loving demeanor that pushes them to keep going. Therefore, we must not become complacent in our obligations. I realize that attending to the emotional needs of students can be extremely taxing. So, do understand that I am not suggesting that you are superhuman or should operate like the energizer bunny. Be intentional in taking the time required to clear your head and decompress, knowing that it is crucial for your success and for all involved.

Last, we are change agents and must quickly forgive and model our expectations for our scholars. For each student that enters your classroom, you want to display an attitude that screams; I am ready to nurture as well as cultivate one of the greatest minds the world has ever known. Examining our hearts is one of the chief investments we will make as teachers because it will force us to make the appropriate adjustments. I promise you that it can only get better when we do. Then, your heart will become more pliable and sensitive to correction. And soon, you will develop the stamina to encounter every challenge head-on.

RELENTLESS

Without a relentless labor of love, the blood flow in our hearts becomes inactive, and we lose the ability to reach our students where they are. As vessels of education, we are to stay the course. Our ability to show up day-in-and-day-out by persevering in a stern, passionate manner is the true definition of being persistent. While many teachers gave up due to societal pressures, others like you searched for reasons to continue. With that investigation came the resilience to overcome every obstacle designed to keep you questioning your significance for showing up to work every day. This is why you should remind yourself often of how important you are. You pushed past mental barriers and emotional setbacks. You released positive words over yourself. Speaking assertively gave you the power to silence the negative voices in your head. Nevertheless, the evidence of your love left an impact on your students that could not be denied and spoke volumes of your strength.

Sometimes, becoming relentless happens when there is opposition. Meeting Timothy and his mom triggered a buried childhood memory that solicited a different response from me, which gave me the courage to reconcile the purpose of my existence. Timothy and many of the families from Head Start pulled deeply on every heartstring I had. It's crazy now, but I needed them because my heart was open to new ideas and ways of being, which allowed me to let my guard down and search for strategies to reach Timothy and the students coming after him. There is strength in permitting yourself to become exposed and utilizing your challenges and struggles to assist someone else. For example, suppose a student is dealing with anxiety due to family drama. In that case, being transparent and sharing a heart story you may have experienced as a child is okay. Or, you may have known of someone who went through something similar. I ask that you be that voice of reassurance by letting your students know they are not alone. Being vulnerable and transparent doesn't mean that you are weak. On the contrary, sharing things you once viewed as embarrassing or shameful takes strength. Displaying a relentless heart shows that you are not only willing to continue in a physical sense but also in a spiritual context. You are not just a teacher; you are all in.

According to the Bible in Revelation 2:19, we hear these words; I know everything you do. I have seen your love, your faith, and your patient endurance. And I can see your constant improvement in all things (NLT). This means that our obligation to the profession of mentorship cannot be compared to that of any other career. With the work of educating comes a weight that compels us to be courageous and not succumb to the pressures that tend to cause a loss of focus. I challenge you to meet every opposition with a steadfast love. Rest in the fact that your faith in what you do has given you the tenacity to not look back. When you've had to stare a child in the face who may have been questioning reasons for existing, your patience allowed you to listen and respond sincerely. Your words provided hope that permitted him to see the silver lining among the clouds of despair. No matter what may lie ahead, know you were created to endure. You have proven this because you are still on the road many have abandoned. Because of your stance, you have prompted other teachers that quit prematurely to question their commitment. Being relentless requires a mindset that emphasizes and embraces the outcomes that will be a success. Your determination promotes relationships that are healthy and grounded in trust. Therefore, I am pushing you to remain unwavering in teaching because children from all walks of life are waiting to cross your doorstep.

Only an unrelenting heart will give you the strength and bravery to stand in the presence of five strands of covid19, masks on and off, and a fluctuation in uncertain mandates. Granted, there is still a ways to go, so hang in there. On the days you feel you are at your wit's end, stop, take a deep breath, and remember your motivation. If that doesn't get your adrenaline flowing and your mind readjusted, it's time to look for a different reset. It could be time to take a vacation or some time off. Let yourself off the hook because you are human, and attending to your needs is okay. Not too long, though, because your students need you, and you need them. Part of being a great teacher is knowing when to say when. Don't give power to anyone who will guilt you into thinking you shouldn't rest or make yourself a priority. Trust me, when it's time for those not in the classroom to take a break, they do so without hesitation. Remember, you are why your students come to school ready to learn. They see you and are encouraged by your conviction to always operate from a sincere place. Not only that, they are motivated by your courage to check yourself and be willing to change. Teachers, sometimes we don't realize how much students need us until we see that we need them too. Lastly, your students admire you for your stamina to finish strong.

With all the changes and complexities involved in today's educational system, I employ you to use the uniqueness of your life as a road map to guide you through the problematic events surrounding teaching. To shed light on what I mean by this, I was a withdrawn student because of my turbulent household environment. That's all I knew; therefore, I shied away from making friends and asserting myself in the learning environment. This definitely affected how I processed, which in turn, made it challenging for me to engage in classroom activities. Everything we go through and experience in life is not just for us. I believe God uses our lives to be a solution to someone else's problem. With that being said, because of my childhood upbringing, I could identify with students who resembled some of the same traits as I did. As a result, I could respond favorably to students who demonstrated emotional setbacks. Of course, every academic school year won't be the same, so find new ways to capture your students' attention. Some years, you will have those tough students; know they are not there by happenstance. There's an unseen explanation for why they are assigned to your class. Remember that your journey will not mirror that of another teacher, so remain confident in your gifts and abilities to accomplish your tasks. It's a fact that no one can beat you at being you, so always stand tall in your capacity to influence those around you. This will help you become more intentional with not overlooking those students that tend to fall by the wayside or have been counted out before being given a chance. Stay in the game; stay in your assigned space. Don't forget to always embrace your authenticity because that's what makes you an exceptional teacher.

Samuel Taylor Coleridge said, "What comes from the heart goes to the heart." This is powerful because of its boomerang effect. In the opening of this chapter, I began with the importance of taking care of your physical heart. I also share the significance of attending to your spiritual heart. Both require a great deal of cultivating because their content affects every part of who we are and those around us. Moving forward, we will examine how our core dictates what comes out of our mouths and its impact on our student's lives.

2

The Mouth of a Teacher

*"Watch your mouth:
The language we use creates the reality we experience."*
—*Michael Hyatt*

As indispensable as our hearts are, the mouth also serves as an elaborate component in holistically caring for our students. However, if used improperly, the mouth poses a threat to those who are under its influence. With that being said, I want to first explain its function. According to MedicineNet.com, the mouth is the upper opening of the digestive tract, beginning with the lips and containing the teeth, gums, and tongue. Once a solid substance enters the mouth, chewing allows it to be broken down and digested. Now that we know its functionality let's highlight its purpose. Kidshealth.org, says its purpose is vital for our ability to speak. As a collaboration, the tongue and teeth assist with forming words by regulating the amount of air that comes out of them.

Not only is it important to understand how words are formed, but equally essential to steward them properly. Words released from an unpruned heart can impair the potential that lies within our students. Therefore, neglecting to take steps to filter emotions like anger, unforgiveness, and pride can impact our young people. Since our hearts are fertile ground for so many feelings, we must diligently address them as soon as we become aware of their destructive effects. If we disregard this obligation, we will give space for them to grow, which will soon spill over into our conversations and influence those around us. We are with our students for a significant portion of their day, more than they are with their parents. Thus, it is safe to assume they will be affected the most. Verbal exchanges are going on all day, so it's important to consider how attentive young ears are. They hear whatever we say and will repeat it. Have you ever heard the expression kids are like sponges because they soak up everything? Whether parents or educators, we know this to be true. Theorists have taught that children are impressionable from birth to five years old and take what we say as authority figures as vital information.

How often have you, as a parent, had your child or children say, "My teacher said…." Or when you tried to correct them, they came back with, "That's not what my teacher said." I rest my case. Students will take what we speak as the "gospel truth," and no one will be able to refute it. As a result, we must be conscious that our words carry weight. If speaking from a heart of mismanaged emotions, it will hinder the forward movement of our mentees. Growing up, I heard people say, "Sticks and stones may break my bones, but words will never hurt me." I don't know where it came from or who thought this was a wise statement, but they didn't understand the gravity of words.

The spoken language can be more destructive than a bodily injury. Now let me explain why I believe this. After you have sustained a physical wound, it heals over time unless there is something else going on that prevents it. However, words aren't just heard and gone when they are articulated. On the contrary, after leaving a person's mouth, they are like seeds planted in fertile soil. Many of those seeds find a resting place in our sensitive space, where they begin to grow due to being watered by our thoughts. Traveling deeper into our inner core, they become overly saturated by our feelings. Soon, they develop into this uncontrollable pile of mixed expressions that we repeatedly replay, creating a perpetual cycle of sustained injury. As a result, it becomes difficult for the wound to heal. Recovery is more difficult every time the scab is pulled off due to words leading to the injury. Visually, words are like nails; they can leave marks even after they are removed.

I hesitated to share this story because I didn't want you to think what we say to our students is mostly negative or degrading. On the contrary, we tend to be very positive toward them for the most part. At any rate, I felt the need to because it rocked me emotionally when I heard it. In August of 2022, I was asked to speak at a Teacher's Retreat. The theme for their school year was "Perspective," and I was to talk from the lens of the student. As I shared what was in my heart, a hand from one of the staff members went up. Paraphrasing, they had to fire a teacher because he was not stewarding his words appropriately. The instructor's words were so bad that the student felt it was necessary to record every insensitive, berating word he said to her. When it was brought to the administration's attention, that child produced a notebook full of his words as proof. I can't imagine the stress she must have felt each time she flipped through the pages of her tablet, rereading what he said and the emotions associated with his verbiage. I surmise she may have needed therapy to assist in coping with the aftermath of that traumatic event.

Listen, not only are wounds inflicted by our mouths but also from the inaudible messages we send. Ever heard of the phrase, "Your actions speak louder than words"? My mom was notorious for using this one when a person's gestures didn't match what their mouth was saying. I recall being in the grocery store with her, and she wanted change for a $20-dollar bill. She asked the clerk if he could break it for her, and he looked at her, sighed, and then stuck his hand out. When we got outside, she mentioned his reluctance, so I asked her how she knew that. She replayed the scenario: the look he gave her, the sigh he made, and then, without any words, he stuck out his hand. All she did was alert me to the many ways we communicate non-verbally. My mom was more concerned with what he did not say as she paid closer attention to his body language. If we're not careful, our actions often reveal what is in our hearts because we say one thing and do the opposite. We can occasionally create undue emotional baggage by responding inappropriately to our deeds, which affects our students. Let me explain; your pupil raises his hand because he has a question. You see his hand, yet instead of positive acknowledgment, you stare intensely and return to your activity. That student slowly lowers his hand and feels dismissed. Though no words were uttered from your lips, the look on your face would suggest you did not want to be bothered. If that didn't hit hard enough, then I have another example.

When I was interning as an undergraduate student in a kindergarten classroom, a little girl needed help with her jacket because the zipper was stuck. The children lined up to go outside, but this problem prevented her from wearing her jacket. Her teacher was standing at the door conversing with a colleague across the hall. When the girl realized she could not fix her coat, she asked for help. I pretended not to be cognizant, but my head turned on a swivel. We all know that teachers, like moms, have eyes in the back of our heads. As instructors, we are constantly multi-tasking. And in this instance, I was lining students up and ensuring they had all gone to the restroom. Sadly, her teacher ignored this little girl and had the nerve to turn her back to her as she continued their conversation. I could not believe she did that. I hope this disappoints you as much as it did me. As she walked away with a fallen countenance and her jacket dragging the floor, I immediately rushed to stand beside her. I asked, "Can I wear your coat outside?" With a wide grin, she said I was too big for it. Her smile was all I needed as a sign that there was still hope for a quick rebound. So, I aided her with getting her zipper loose. Looking back at that moment, I am grateful that I was present and willing to help. Look, I am not trying to bash any teacher because we all have had days when we might not feel our little ones. But, I am saying that we must do better with addressing the silent cries and the loud pleas for assistance. Had she taken a second to address the baby's concern over her jacket, the outcome would have been so different in the eyes of this student. This teacher's demeanor shaped that young person's image and how she would potentially view her in the future. Honestly, I can't say this enough, our communication must be intentional, whether verbal or non-verbal; it has the propensity to change our interactions with the lives we are supposed to nurture daily.

I am reminded of my early years of teaching. My boss strongly encouraged me to take a seminar on communication because she had received a few complaints from my parents. I thought, who me? I could not recall any interactions where I said something rude or unprofessional. I registered, but I did not want to. Oddly enough, I enjoyed the first day and learned some interesting facts. However, on the second day, it occurred to me that it was not what I was saying that rubbed my parents the wrong way; it was what I was not saying. I was intrigued to learn that 70 to 93 percent of all communication is non-verbal. My body language, facial expressions, eye contact, and posture spoke louder. Laughing at myself, I was famous for using facial expressions to communicate what I could not say. My husband often said, "Fix your face." Most of the time, I blew him off as if he had the problem, not me. Of course, I could not see what I was doing, but I knew deep down inside he was speaking the truth. Information shared at the seminar made me realize that my body gestures exposed my feelings. It was so much a part of who I was. I had not considered how intimidating or threatening the folding of my arms while talking with a parent could have been perceived. I needed to reset the way I interacted with them and others. I worked to improve, ensuring my words lined up with my actions. Was it easy? Absolutely not! Worth it, without a doubt!!

As you refine your communication skills, know that you will grow in ways you never thought possible; I did. I learned to breathe and shift my body when I felt tense or wanted to say something that would sting. In addition, I also made it a point to cup my hands when having difficulty talking with certain adults or challenging students. But, again, we know that students are always listening even when their focus appears elsewhere. In fact, they have perfected the craft of ear hustling. Ear hustling is what we older folk call eavesdropping. Listen, my three-and-a-half-year-old grandson can be in the living room, and I can be in the kitchen talking with his mom, and out of nowhere, he will respond to something I said to her. Their ears are everywhere. So, not only are we held liable for what we say to and around them, but also for what we model in front of them.

SCRIPTURE

Ephesians 4:29 says, "Don't use foul or abusive language. Let everything you say be good and helpful so that your words will be an encouragement to those who hear them" (NLT). Hence, we must amend our words and be mindful of our tone. We change lives - literally.

When we really think about it, God trusts us to care for his most prized possession, children. Wow, what confidence He must have in educators. Therefore, we cannot afford to blow our representation by misappropriating our authority by saying harmful words or modeling demeaning actions. Students are vulnerable. As far-fetched as this may sound, many students depend on us to protect them and come to their rescue if needed. How indicting would it be for a child looking for a safe place to find the same abusive atmosphere they have at home, in our classes? This wouldn't be good at all. By no means am I suggesting that every word vocalized be laced with honey; however, I am advocating for a greater effort to be made in our ability to refrain from using words that cause students to feel devalued. Our language should incite emotions that push them to put their best foot forward. Being an educator is a personal journey that changes the lives of many. When they enter your room, you want their expectations to be high, with the anticipation of having their best day.

Therefore, I pray you will not identify with instructors who tend to put their students down through derogatory comments. As I am much older now, whenever I talk about this one elementary teacher, I still feel the abrasiveness of her words. My experience with her left me wondering how she could teach for so long. In my mind, it would have appeared that teachers were not held accountable for what they said to us. But this generation of students is not as tolerant. Many are angry and have little to no regard for authority; this is why you should be sensitive to what you say. Kindness doesn't cost a thing. Thus, it takes more energy to be unkind and use unloving words than it does to do the complete opposite, which is my logic behind this narrative.

I need to share this memory with the hope of helping a fellow educator. I was excited to enter the fourth grade until I met Ms. P. She was one of the grumpiest people I had ever seen in my young life. She would sit at her desk, looking over her glasses and giving orders. She rarely smiled and hardly ever used kind words. I do not recall her saying good morning as we entered her room. I did not like going to her class because she was more of a taskmaster than a teacher. Not only did I view her as overbearing, but she also took pleasure in calling us names. Her favorite name to call us if we gave a wrong answer or said something she did not like was "Dumb Dora."

At nine, I certainly did not know what a Dumb Dora was, nor had I heard anyone being called that before. Moreover, where I am in life now, I still do not know what or who that person is. My mom was good at calling names but had never used that before. Nevertheless, I watched my peer's countenance change whenever she said it. Heads would hang low, and tears would sometimes pool in the corner of their eyes. I truly disliked her for that. We were there to learn not to be called names or made to feel stupid. Besides being called names, it was more disturbing to me that she did not care if she hurt our feelings as she displayed a stoic, hard-core demeanor. Then, to add insult to our verbal injuries, she would make us stand outside her door until we pulled it together if we could not rebound quickly enough from her damaging comments.

Undoubtedly, she is not alone as it pertains to being unable to leave baggage at home or outside her classroom door. Again, though, I empathize with those who have rough days. Nevertheless, I am not a proponent of educators calling students out of their names. Nor is it acceptable to think that we can use words unrelated to building confidence in our students. At the end of the day, we must still consider our environment and make wise choices concerning our verbal exchanges. When you feel overwhelmed, I would ask that you put yourself in a timeout. There is simply nothing wrong with it. When I taught my first Pre-K class of ten, I used to. If you need more than a timeout, take a walk, or have someone step into your room so you can take a minute or two to decompress.

There were days my 2 ½ - 3-year-olds had me climbing the ceiling. Finally, I had to get somewhere and sit my butt down. I needed a break to breathe. Though young and often rambunctious, I knew some days I tended to overlook that they were little human beings with feelings. As those in charge, our position dictates we become more delicate because we don't know their struggles; they want to know that we have their best interest at heart. As young impressionable learners, I think they would get excited to see you put yourself in a little chair and sit there until you regroup. That act alone would change their perspective of who you are and potentially open the door for building a stronger rapport with them.

Once you demonstrate that you can be a kid, too, I promise you will be viewed as the cool teacher they can relate to. No matter how stern we may be, every educator desires to be revered as someone their students can admire. Think about it for a minute. You stated that you began this voyage of educating because you wanted to be set apart from the status quo teacher. With every growing year, you saw the need for change and knew the value you would add. Maybe, you saw the broken youth in your neighborhood. Or, you thought about those who would be rejected because of where they came from, and you felt a strong sense of obligation to be their change agent. Perhaps, you considered your words of affirmation as a stabilizer for those headed in a downward spiral. There's no doubt that when you become weary, you wonder if you should continue; of course, you should. Just a few weeks ago, you encountered a student who is now doing well because of your strength and aspiration to be accessible. Celebrate how you have grown in your ability to speak life over situations that seemed bleak. You have become that mouthpiece that has embraced the significance of crafting words with intentionality to build confident and thriving students. During critical times, you used words that provided hope. There were even situations where you did not say anything, yet the outcome was positive because of your presence. And as a result, your students gained the courage to complete the school year. It would be careless of me to downplay your sacrifices throughout your tenure, so I won't. Instead, I commend you for permitting yourself to alter your perspective about strategies and how you approach each new school term. When we think differently about our influence, communicating becomes more meticulous. Knowing how this impacts our students, our words become more heart-centered instead of mindless chatter. More importantly, we must adopt a philosophy that reminds us that our conversations should inspire and create atmospheres that spark perseverance in our scholars. Nothing is more gratifying than modifying our thought patterns and fine-tuning our words. Making mental adjustments before opening our mouths to speak is worth it. Moreover, feeling good about our words and actions is even more critical. Repeat after me, "I'm really good at this!" Believe it because you are.

Let's Pray:

Father, I thank you for the ability to use my mouth to speak to those you have placed in my life. Help me be mindful of my words and remind me of my responsibility to create self-sufficient individuals as I continue to guard my heart and mouth. As I progress through this journey, it reminds me that my non-verbal actions can be as detrimental as loose words. Thank you for the grace and mercy to become better and more intentional in representing myself.
In Jesus' Name, Amen.

RECALIBRATION

Thank you for praying that prayer. Sometimes taking a quick second to whisper a prayer can refocus you. Although easier said than done, shifting a mouth mindset requires discipline. Trust me; I am not saying to do anything I have not done myself. It is a process of working through familiar things. When we think about how words have negatively influenced our life, how much more of an impression will they leave on our young ones? Of course, constructive words build, but destructive ones leave casualties along the way. My classmates and I needed an advocate with our fourth-grade teacher because she lacked the tools for self-control as it pertained to what came out of her mouth. It's quite sad when an instructor is not open to transformation. When they are not, it will hinder their ability to recalibrate effectively. I believe successful teachers are bold enough to acknowledge the severity of their words and are willing to improve. From what I am sensing, you are among those that have accepted the challenge to refocus for a greater outcome. You have come too far to think about passing the baton to someone else before finishing what you started. If you survived the trauma of Covid19 and depression, you can certainly adjust how you converse with your students.

Get out of your head; you've done the hard part. I commend you for the significant strides you made to stay on track. One of your greatest successes was disregarding emotions that triggered quick-tempered responses. Now, make it a point to manage your thoughts carefully because they will determine what you say. You have proven that you have the resilience to speak favorably. As you continue to build the momentum to keep going, know that your words will leave an affirmative mark that cannot be erased.

RELENTLESS

Subsequently, leaving a lasting imprint on your students will produce a perpetual effect for ages to come. Therefore, we must always be aware of the power of our mouths, or we risk potentially creating paths for our students they were not meant to travel. In other words, we begin to speak about things that can alter the trajectory of their lives. Ponder the potential setback they could experience at the expense of our misguided words. Assessing some of the encounters you may have had with other teachers may help you to become more sensitive in censoring your dialogue. Hence, my fourth-grade teacher will forever serve as a reminder for me.

The better we see the big picture, the more strategic we become in remaining consistent. Our ability to stay connected and unwavering builds the stamina to keep going. You were born to do this. Sure, it can be challenging; however, your feelings should not outweigh your commitment to your promise. Be relentless! You vowed to be what your kids needed as a means of making it impossible for them to fail. Say this aloud, "I will not leave my post until it is time. I am in it for the long haul."

Didn't that feel good? It should have. You managed to stay relevant during your many challenges and all you had to contend with. I know it took fortitude. In addition, you had to pace yourself while pursuing academic excellence. You kept a goal before you and prioritized it - great job. As a result of your attitude conversion, I am confident your dialogue exchanges are softer, and your heart has become more pliable to the needs of your learners. Your approach has taken a step in the right direction, and you have become more intimate in recognizing their potential. Again, great job realizing you are not just a teacher – you are so much more!

You Are Not Just A Teacher; You Are So Much More!
Darlene Northam

So, find your inspiration – that person or thing that makes your approach relentless. I did when I worked in a deprived community. When I first started, I asked myself why I was there. I soon learned that many of those students needed to see the drive I had to not give up on them. I was determined they would leave my classroom academically and emotionally sound. Every time I saw a face, it reminded me why I could not quit. All I kept hearing was, "If they fail, so do you." Timothy aided me with the inspiration I needed to keep going. Yes, he reminded me of my self-imposed limitations when things got stressful. This insight gave me the knowledge to overcome the word barriers I used to hinder me from trusting in myself. Your purpose and destiny are connected to you becoming vulnerable enough to expose your heart. Be willing to let go and pour yourself entirely into your scholars' lives. This nourishment is needed to guide you through obstacles and will cause you to thrive. That next student is waiting.

One day, you will have a Shaniqua who will benefit from your relentlessness. Do not be intimidated to speak words that will drive her to persevere in the face of opposition. Your exchanges will push her to excel. The pride you will experience watching her finish will be invaluable. I commend you because you did not make it about you. Instead, you decided to be a beckon of light for those students who encountered some pretty dark moments. Your resilience has given you tough skin. Make no mistake about it; your students will see it and hear it as you advocate for their success. It will not matter what anyone else has to say or think because you are that credible other. You are their voice! Whew! This accomplishment is noteworthy, so continue to forge ahead and be that influencer.

Your tenacity to press and not give in to discouragement has reinforced your desire to leave a positive stamp on your kids. As a result, young minds are waiting to come into your classroom that you have yet to meet. The truth is that your interactions with them will be centered on more than academic content because of the relationships you have fostered. As a result of those connections, other educators will embrace the significance of establishing a genuine rapport with their students and families. In turn, you will create a perpetual cycle of stories that will be shared for generations to come.

I say this because my educational journey took the most amazing turn when I began teaching at Head Start. During this time, I realized how much God had placed within me that I had not tapped into. I was in a space where I had no choice but to rely on my life and academic experiences. Not only were the interactions with my students a game changer for them but for me as well. Let me explain. My mouth echoed words that sparked growing confidence in my students. Over time, that push challenged them to do their best. Interestingly enough, my words didn't just carry weight with them but my co-workers as well. During staff meetings,

I discovered they were listening to my voice too. I felt like the vintage E. F. Hutton commercial; when I spoke, people listened.

This was a sobering encounter as it demonstrated how powerful my words were. But, more importantly, it encouraged me to continue to make good word choices because of how others responded. As someone who believes in pushing other teachers to be their best selves, I challenge you to say to your students what you would like said to you. With each passing day, it will become easier to say purposeful words. Not only that, but you will also find that your words will create a positive classroom experience. So, be that consistent presence in the lives of your students. Do not allow external pressures to keep you from opening your mouth to speak affirming words that will shape your pupils' minds and the words they speak as well.

Hear me when I say you have shown great tenacity by showing up each day and displaying a heart for your students. Though the road has been a little rocky occasionally, you have managed to stay the course. Kudos to you! Your drive is unmatched, and I mean it. Remember this; your reward will be greater than any monetary compensation. Trust me; I am not discounting the relevance of feeling valued financially. Instead, I am saying that your decision to remain dedicated to enhancing your students' future is based on your compassion for them.

You Are Not Just A Teacher; You Are So Much More!
Darlene Northam

THE DEMONSTRATION OF OUR WORDS

"One's eyes are what one is; one's mouth is what one becomes," is a quote from John Galsworthy. The demonstration of your words has shown them how to endure. Aside from this, they will learn how to encourage themselves when situations look dismal. Every verbal deposit you make will, in turn, prepare them for something greater. Moreover, your words will continue to grow in their hearts and sprout new aspirations as they mature. Isn't this the reason you teach? Your goal is to see them overcome obstacles that once hindered them as they progress through education. Remember, we must attend to our words with sensitivity. Not only will we become what we say, but so will our students.

Now, stay confident, and do not stop loving what you do!

3

The Eyes of a Teacher

"The tongue may hide the truth, but the eyes—never!"
—Mikhail Bulgakov,

By comparison, our eyes are equally as important as our mouths in tailoring our successes. They complement one another because what our eyes see, our mouths will speak. Growing up, I used to hear that our eyes are the windows to our souls, and beauty is in the eye of the beholder. Per these statements, the eye is valuable. Of course, we do not realize this when we are young. We have been taught to see with our eyes only, but nothing relative to using them to distinguish situations or circumstances. However, life teaches us the importance of paying attention to our surroundings because our perception is our reality. My point is two people can witness the same occurrence, and each will have a different interpretation of what they saw. Therefore, it becomes imperative that we use our eyes to discern and also make assessments concerning life's challenges.

You Are Not Just A Teacher; You Are So Much More!
Darlene Northam

What do I mean? I believe there are two ways we can see things. One is by using the naked eye and the other through the lenses of our heart, which solicits an attitude of sensitivity. The latter allows us to be more aware of our youth's mental and emotional state. In addition, we develop a better understanding of becoming more accepting of their differences as we partner with them in the learning process. As allies, we demonstrate a self-awareness that keeps us grounded in how we speak, see, and interact with them. Seeing them through a compassionate eye causes us to display a more conscious level of accountability. It petitions empathy and compels us to become less judgmental.

Before we go deeper into the subject of our eyes, let's identify their purpose and function. According to an online source, Human Eye-Definition, Structure, Function, Parts, Diagram, the eye is important. So much so that it is considered one of the most multifaceted sense organs in the human body; they assist with our ability to visualize objects and light awareness. They also help us distinguish color and gravity sensitivity. Our eyes operate like a camera. "Much like the electronic device, the human eye also focuses and lets in light to produce images." Although our eyes take pictures and can recall what they have seen, in conjunction, our heart gives us the perception to comprehend what our eyes can't.

Listen, as we meet our students, it will become necessary to establish meaningful bonds to help us perceive the intricate details of their character. And doing so will speak volumes and send a message that we value who they are. Whatever caliber we set for our pupils determines their merit in our view of them. Our relationship's net worth increases as we learn complex information about them. It provides us with a deeper understanding of their makeup.

I know asking you to extend yourself beyond what you already do may be more than you are willing to give. First, we talked about our hearts, then our mouths, and now I am stretching you even more with sight; I know, I know. However, I am not talking about identifying them by name but rather by personality, habits, and interests, which I believe is one of the ways to address verbal and non-verbal cues for help. As professionals who save lives, we cannot afford to operate haphazardly. Our students are too valuable and deserve the best we have to offer. For example, when a student is going through a situation at home, with a parent not being available to provide support, your consistent hands-on interactions will provide that student with what is needed. In addition, your reassurance and intuitiveness will aid your students in pursuing their goals.

I want to share a situation that escaped me initially because I only observed using surface vision. It was during my second year of working with an impoverished community when a small-framed, soft-spoken little boy with braids entered my room. His long mane caught my attention because, at first glance, I thought he was a girl. Then I noticed his clothes and shoes; he was standoffish and withdrawn. Some students reached for his hand to play with him, but he declined their advances. In fact, after a week or so, he still did not interact with many of his classmates, although he did have one or two that he gravitated to. Initially, I assumed it was first-time classroom jitters. But, hoping he would soon let his guard down and join some of the activities, his behavior remained the same. As a result, I began to take mental notes.

It was not until mealtimes that I noticed a different type of demeanor. Each day, as the other children sat talking to one another and asking for more food, he would not say a word. During our mealtimes, we implemented what was known as "Family Style Dining," which required the staff to sit at the table and eat with their scholars. These moments were used to encourage our mentees to use their manners in addition to teaching table etiquette. Because many children had poor diets, we modeled how important it was to eat everything on your plate. Once done, they were allowed to ask for seconds if more was available. On the days we served something they liked, they licked the plates clean and wasted no time asking for more. However, this boy would eat everything on his plate in one gobble. Frightened that he would choke, I would tell him to slow down. After he had finished, he watched his peers eat until they were full. He never asked for seconds but would not leave when he was done. This puzzled me because he would cry when it was time to transition. It didn't matter whether it was breakfast, lunch, or snack time.

After replaying the mealtimes and his reactions, I perceived he was still hungry but would not ask for additional food. So, the next day, I decided to test my theory. It was during breakfast, and after he ate his first plate of food, I asked if he wanted more. He looked at me with sadness but said nothing. His brown eyes were screaming help me; I am hungry.

I had a lightbulb moment as I saw in his eyes what his mouth failed to utter. Without reservation, I gave him a second helping, and again he seemed to swallow everything whole. When he got up from the table this day, he looked thick like the Pillsbury Dough Boy. It was the first time he did not cry when he left his seat. From that day on, the shame of asking for more food was a thing of the past. He knew I cared and would not scold him for eating what he wanted or needed, for that matter. His well-being was important to me. My ability to ascertain his hunger pangs through an empathetic eye showed him that he mattered. Though I felt good about resolving that dilemma, I was still concerned about why he was so hungry when he came to school. It wasn't until I had to do the home visit that I got my answer. His mom was receiving food stamps (government assistance) for him and his three siblings; however, she mismanaged them for personal reasons.

You probably think I was doing the most; however, it was disheartening that this child's essential needs were unmet. As educators, we know how important eating is in the learning process. Studies have shown that children are more apt to do better in school with a healthy diet. In addition, it's no secret that when a child is hungry, it prevents him from focusing because all he can think about is food. Let's be honest; many of us sometimes struggle to stay on task when hungry. Why would it be any different for them?

Educating our students is a small fraction of what we do. Moreover, we see so much more than we often care to address, which is why some of us do what we do. So, when I've been told that I am extra, I take it as a compliment. I have not limited myself to just teaching because we encounter a plethora of unmet needs daily. After dealing with the mealtime issue, I felt obligated to intervene again. I couldn't disregard his disheveled appearance. He often came to school in clothes that were too big and dirty. From the wrinkles and smell, he appeared to have slept in them. If you could only see what I saw. Some may contend it wasn't a serious matter, but I disagree. In my mind, it was much bigger than what he wore. I watched his countenance drop when he entered the classroom, where most of his peers dressed fashionably. It was more noticeable during circle time. If he was standing next to a classmate dressed nicely, he would eyeball that student up and down and sometimes switch positions. Witnessing this prompted me to assist the only way I knew how.

Watching a four-year-old display that type of demeanor caused my heart to hurt for him, so I purchased a few outfits. This is not to stroke me or employ any accolades. For those of us who empathize with some of the challenges our students face, we don't think twice about intervening. When his mom came to pick him up that afternoon, I gave her the bag containing the items. He did not wear them right away. I assumed she had sold them too. Yep, I sure did! Don't judge me; I am just being transparent. At any rate, about a week or so later, he came in with his head held high and the biggest smile I had ever seen on him. To my surprise, his mom had dressed him in one of the outfits, and he wore it proudly. Until then, he hadn't said much nor displayed any type of assertiveness in class. However, something triggered a response from him that I had not witnessed the whole time he had been in my class. He was not the same. It was as if he felt a sense of validation and belonging. His behavior resembled an evolving butterfly. He looked good, and he knew it. He identified with some of the other well-dressed students. I could not keep him quiet because he was excited.

Consequently, during center time, he played with two children he had not before. After a few minutes, he stood beside me and gently grabbed my hand, again, a new behavior. I felt every ounce of his emotions in that touch. I noted this change, watching him as he talked more and interacted with his classmates. There was a level of self-confidence being displayed, and it filled the room. As I said earlier, I don't believe the new clothes sparked the gleam in his eyes. It was my ability to discern a child's longing to be seen and acknowledge him by responding to his inaudible cry. As a misnomer, adults used to say, "Children should be seen and not heard." I hope and pray none of you will ever ascribe to that foolishness. Children should be heard and seen; otherwise, their situations, issues, or concerns will not be addressed. Moving on, lest I get stuck in my emotions.

Spending personal funds to help a child wasn't new for me. But this time, it felt different. This student's gratitude was genuine and heartfelt. Writing about this has me reliving that encounter, and I appreciate having the privilege of knowing him. Thinking about my journey is important to me because of the former students I bump into occasionally. Some of them were no older than three when I taught them. A few recognize me. However, the students I had a more intimate relationship with have not forgotten our interactions. They recalled the smallest details about me acknowledging them from the other students. I don't know how, but one student said he even knew the exact words I spoke to him the day he said he didn't want to come back to school. What a significant impact we can ultimately have on our scholars. Although they are much older, I still get a hug, which solidifies that the extra time and financial sacrifices were all worth it. I am certain this has happened to some of you as well. It's the best experience in the world to admit that our influence is still felt years later.

Listen, our eyes are vital in seeing who our students truly are. Undoubtedly, seeing them at-a-glance may cause us to miss a great deal concerning their makeup and who they are. The reason we miss intricate details is due to us being preoccupied with the affairs of the job. Without digging deeper, we tend to focus on what students may wear, how they speak, or who their parents are. All this does is cause us to form opinions and make superficial assumptions, which are not beneficial for the student. Therefore, we must engage them in utilizing our visual perception so that our exchanges are intentional and purpose-driven. Once we tap into a deliberate mindset when considering those we have in our classroom, we become privy to those hidden hurts and disappointments. Some of those concealed displeasures are parents not being home to help with homework. Or parents not being available to do fun things. The biggest discontent I perceived was many students felt like their parents ignored them. To this point, one day, I had a little girl say, "My mom doesn't tell me that I'm pretty." In spite of the nice clothes, well-groomed hair, and articulate speech, our children are screaming to be noticed. When everything on the outside is intact, our vision can become obscured and blind us, preventing us from seeing past what we need to see.

Having eyes to witness what is not visibly apparent can be extremely difficult because some students have become proficient at hiding their internal dysfunction. Hence, we should develop ways to see holistically who we have in our classrooms. Ascertaining key things about them is so important. Each year, I did an "All About Me" exercise sheet. I wanted to know interesting facts about them. It gave me information they may not have shared in an open forum. And it gave me glimpses of positive and negative character traits. I used this form at every grade level, even my 2 ½ and 3-year-old students. Of course, the parents completed the sheet for the younger age groups. The sheet was a great segue into establishing relationships with my students and their families. Obtaining nuggets of vital information early on allowed me to deal with some of the challenges initially and not wait until they were spiraling out of control near the end of the school year.

Furthermore, we can also take the information gathered to create a consciousness of the potential within each student. Sometimes, we fail to employ the knowledge we receive to encourage or guide them toward purpose. This can be accomplished if we can distinguish their inner workings. For example, some children are shy and withdrawn, which means they may not come out and volunteer. As well they may not engage in conversation during moments that have been designated for that purpose. That being said, we must be observant of silent gestures and body language. Our role as educators spreads far beyond the scope of reading, writing, and math. I know this because of the additional time and energy we spend addressing hidden pain.

Case in point. One year I assisted a school board member and friend with tutoring. She assigned me math SOL remediation for fourth graders. I met a cute, outspoken, bossy nine-year-old girl the first week. She always said something negative about the lesson and refused to participate. I first thought she was disrespectful and had little regard for authority. When she spoke, it was like an adult talking. Not only did I hear what she was saying, but I also observed her body language, her facial expressions, and tone. She appeared angry about something, and I couldn't understand why. So, she and I talked briefly about her behavior after math class. At first, she hesitated to be honest about her feelings until I shared what I sensed. Fighting with everything inside her to not let me see her cry, she turned her head slightly in the opposite direction. Her faint turn was just enough for me to notice her tears pooling. Instead of sharing that her mom refused to buy school supplies, she pretended not to care. She downplayed having the necessary supplies for school. Our heart-to-heart showed me a soft place within her that many probably dismissed because of her hard-outward demeanor.

Nevertheless, her transparency compelled me to be creative. That evening after school, I stopped by Walmart to purchase supplies to construct a makeshift store. I could have just given her the items, which may have caused friction between her and Mom, so I allowed her to earn them. The next day, I got to the classroom a little earlier than usual to set up everything. When the students came in, they were utterly surprised, especially her. I excitedly explained the assignment and provided details on how they could earn money to buy whatever they desired from the store. On that day, I made a friend for life and gained respect not just from her but the others as well. Hope became possible. She realized that things could change suddenly, and because a situation may start one way does not mean it has to end the same way. Had I not been able to differentiate that there was more going on in that child's life, I would have potentially missed an opportunity to meet a need that changed her perspective as well as the outcome. No one would have ever guessed, by looking at her, that she had the potential to be a straight-A student. Although she was an astute learner, it was camouflaged by embarrassment and denial.

As mentors, we must see our students through empathic lenses. And, in doing so, we will be able to speak words that give them hope. Subsequently, we may be our students' only advocates for optimism.

SCRIPTURE

Our eyes not only reveal what we see but also who we are. Like our students, we try to hide behind what is visible, our makeup, hairstyles, and clothing, for fear of rejection or being judged. However, there are times when others will uncover those things we are powerless to conceal. Sooner or later, an discerning eye will see past what the natural eye can comprehend. I believe this is why some students have difficulty looking their teachers in the eyes when conversing. In any case, I trust that Matthew 6:22 (TPT) helps us better understand the content. It states that the eyes of your spirit allow revelation light to enter your being. If your heart is unclouded, the light floods in! In essence, what the text is sharing is this. If the core is pure, without ill intent towards another, then that is what your students will see in you.

I used to ask God to allow me to see people the way He sees them. Now that I look back, I was not ready for his answer. When I initially asked, my eyes required me to view my students and others with a compassionate eye, which is how God views us. No matter how long you have been an educator, it's necessary to observe your pupils in a way they feel like they are the apple of your eye. To *see* them adds value to the relationship. Never take for granted that our students have become experts at camouflage.

This scriptural text helps us to understand that being more concerned with looks can be deceiving and cause us to make decisions about our students and others that may prove to be unfavorable. With this in mind, I encourage us to treat them as precious cargo, observing every detail about them. It doesn't matter what they look like on the outside because they will only present what they think we want to see, something like a false reality. Society, however, has conditioned us to believe that what we witness is more important than the truth. Unfortunately, this hinders our students, creating a space that does not allow them to be themselves. When this happens, we potentially co-sign and permit them to wear masks, making it difficult to identify their genuineness. According to the scripture, it doesn't matter what our outer persona displays because our hearts will always reveal our intent. Hence, we should not be so quick to jump to a conclusion after our first interaction. But, no matter how skilled our students are at presenting false narratives, their hearts will expose them every time. Therefore, we must condition our sight to obtain the ability to separate what is not visible to gain a better understanding.

Furthermore, our viewpoint of situations will also be displayed in our actions. Everything that goes through our eye gate is processed from a place of innocence or a place that has become contaminated by this world's destructive influences. Let's use this example. A student enters the classroom early in the morning. He's disheveled in his appearance, moving slowly and somewhat disoriented. Despite his feelings, he comes to class, sits, and places his head on the desk. His teacher's first remarks are, "If you had gone to bed last night instead of hanging out in the streets with your hoodlum's friends, you wouldn't be tired this morning." By her accusation, you would think she had an inside track to his whereabouts the night before. I venture to say that she did not. Therefore, her assumption was based on a viewpoint filtered through a tainted set of lenses. As a result, she could not perceive that her student was incapable of being his best because he had spent most of the night at the hospital with his mom, who had suffered a stroke. Again, our vision reflects the good and the bad, demonstrated by the words spoken from our mouths.

If I may, in my own words, share the B portion of 1 Samuel 16:7; it says it like this, we spend lots of time and energy looking at people's outward appearance. That does not impress God, and it shouldn't impress us. But God is more concerned with what's in a person's heart. Deciphering what is happening in a student's life will take intentional practice. As professionals, having an observant eye will often alert us to the illusion that all is well when many of our scholars are one situation away from having a major setback. Our ability to differentiate what is behind the disguise is crucial because their cries are not audible yet painful in nature. Sometimes, our scholars cannot articulate the trauma they may be experiencing. It is during those times we must be open to interpreting what they are displaying by their actions. Essentially, we become that light that uncovers those things they try to suppress for fear of being judged. When we take the time to examine situations from a healthy heart space, our vision is less blurred. In fact, our eyes become wide open and more receptive to separating the discomfort and frustration that is not so obvious to the naked eye. Allowing oneself to become vulnerable to what our hearts show us requires a different kind of commitment. I want to say it's declaring that you're all in. I can't help but wonder what would happen if we asked God to open the eyes of our hearts so that we may be enlightened and flooded by the light of the Holy Spirit. I believe God would honor our request and show us not only the concerns of our students but also those unseen things we fail to recognize about ourselves. I pray for the state of our hearts to become illuminated by that truth and alter our perspective. So, instead of seeing the glass half empty, we will see the glass half full. Doing so provides opportunities for us to conduct honest assessments of our interactions with our students, giving us the necessary skill set to correct our sight for sharper perception.

Seeing clearly requires us to constantly seek God for revelation, so He can show us what we tend to ignore about ourselves. As a matter of fact, our issues and prejudices are not hidden from him. Making this a part of our daily regimen will yield a completely different outlook causing us to produce authentic relationships with our students. That being said, the students we interact with will expect integrity from us. And they should because we are assigned to ensure they are academically sound and equipped to become productive citizens after they leave us. When they become successful businessmen and women living their best lives, they will remember our lessons.

Walking down memory lane, I recall teaching K 2 ½ - K 3 students. It's kind of funny now. However, they made me feel like a superhero. I don't know why those children thought I knew everything and could do even more. Somedays, they thought I was like Clark Kent, Superman, leaping buildings in a single bound while rescuing them from anything designed to harm them. To my point, we have been graced with versatility. No one else can do it like us and be as effective. Honestly, we meet more needs and save more lives than any medical professional ever will. It's more than a job; it's a call.

You Are Not Just A Teacher; You Are So Much More!
Darlene Northam

Let's pray:

Father, we come asking that you open our eyes to the things that are hidden in the lives of our students. We ask that you not only reveal those things but also show us who we are and the things that are deeply rooted in us. God, allow the scales to fall from our eyes so we can begin to discern and not form judgments as it pertains to the situations concerning what is happening in their lives. We want to become better stewards of their destiny and deliberate in our interactions with them.
In Jesus' Name, Amen.

RECALIBRATION

If you are like me, you're probably wondering how to transition from how you have been conditioned to look at things. It is not easy, mainly because of how each of us has been cultured in our upbringing but also because of societal influences. Either we grew up with positive guidance and consistent support from family and loved ones, or like me, we were surrounded by those who only saw the negative outcome. With the insensitivity came words that constantly incited fear, which caused self-esteem problems. Coupled with the lack of support, I struggled to maintain relevance in a community of prejudices.

Over time, though, I discovered that one of the most effective ways to begin looking at things differently was to realize that my vision needed adjusting. Subsequently, I chose to posture myself so I could see more distinctly. As a result, I became more intentional in monitoring the words coming out of my mouth. Getting us to change our perspective concerning long-held viewpoints can occasionally be challenging. Nevertheless, it is the responsibility of the nurturer to build up, not tear down. Quite often, we react instead of responding. According to the Merriam-Webster Dictionary, the word react means to act in opposition to a force of influence. Our charge is to allow our eyes to adjust or adapt before speaking. What do I mean? After seeing a situation that may not be to our liking, we should take the time to investigate other possible results before jumping to a critical conclusion. I am also talking to myself because conversion did not happen immediately. We must consider facial expressions, body language, and tone. To this end, we miss so much initially due to our inability to train our eyes to notice key red flags during our first scan. Moreover, many of us get so distracted by colors, smells, and background noises that we neglect to focus on everything concerning that student.

Therefore, I encourage you to evaluate why your sight is blurred. Ask yourself why you are so quick to assess an event negatively instead of positively. Document how often you use undesirable vocabulary to describe what you observe. Then make it a point to become more disciplined in training your eyes to comprehend from a heart of hopefulness, so you can begin to speak promising conclusions. Your students will appreciate you for it. More importantly, you will be on a path of envisioning greater for your students.

RELENTLESS

Never let it be said that you are not built for the challenges you've faced and will continue to face. You are phenomenal because you have been assigned to charter a course for the lives of children. You have overcome obstacles in many ways by allowing yourself to become pliable. It's certainly not easy to pivot midstride and do something completely foreign as a means of helping students thrive. I honor you for continuing to look for that silver lining that pushes you toward excellence. Don't stop recalling the first day you took your post with the hopes of creating an atmosphere for scholars to excel. The enthusiasm that you possess is contagious. Other educators need what you have and count on your strength and dedication to help them navigate the rough patches. Teachers like you are not celebrated enough. Therefore, it becomes imperative that you affirm the greatness that resides within you. The magnitude of your steadfastness is unmatched. You already know you are more than your assigned title because you never missed a beat amid an almost three-year pandemic.

On the days when quitting was written all over your face, you hung in there, so I got to give you your props. I challenge you to see yourself as your mentees see you. Without a shadow of a doubt, they acknowledge your resilience and commitment.

You Are Not Just A Teacher; You Are So Much More!
Darlene Northam

Among other things, you have been an avid supporter. The truth is they also witnessed you giving your best even when you knew there were those in opposition to you succeeding. I don't know you personally, but I believe I am connected to your heart which has been displayed by your survivorship. I have discerned your willpower to stay the course because you trust that every child deserves a chance to prove they matter. Real talk: all they want is an opportunity to be recognized. Not only does every child deserve a chance to achieve, but also a teacher who celebrates them.

Because of your strong constitution to finish what you've started, I trust that your heart can embrace each student's uniqueness to grow beyond your level of comprehension. As a result of your expansion, I hope your mouth will speak life to every student in your sphere of influence, and they will walk with confidence. Also, I trust that your eyes will forecast the possibilities, not the obvious. As you progress, your tenacity to overcome will propel you into a season of your career that will set a precedence for other teachers. Do not discount who you are, and certainly, don't allow anyone else to do it. From one educator to another, keep plugging, striving, and affirming that your ability to change lives rests in your confidence to detect hidden things.

4

The Ears of a Teacher

"What is important is not what you hear said; it's what you observe."
— *Michael Connelly*

Earlier, we talked about our heart being the essence of who we are and how critical engaging our mouths and eyes is in our educating process. As vital as these three anatomical parts are, our ears are equally important. Until now, I am not sure how many of us have cared or thought to relate the condition of our hearts to the ripple effect it can have on our conversations and how we hear. For example, a student said, "I neglected to bring in my assignment because I didn't feel like doing it." But you actually discerned that I didn't do my assignment because I didn't have the means to purchase the materials. Think about it, when a heart processes using an intentional and sympathetic ear, it allows one to hear what is not spoken. Thus, the content of our hearts will significantly affect how we function. Whatever unfavorable characteristics we tend to disguise will soon manifest in our interactions and cripple our relationships with our students.

Consequently, a noble heart will be thoughtful and hear the positive in that which is spoken. In contrast, a tainted heart will only hear the negative. Writing this book opened my mind to the level of productivity we gain when we rely on and utilize all of our senses in the instruction process.

Hopefully, we have gained more insight into how fundamental it is to activate our faculties encompassing our heart, mouth, eyes, and now ears. As we proceed, I want us to look at how our ears function in the holistic scheme of things. The ears are a complex system that incorporates three intricate sections and the brain for hearing. Britannica.com says the human ear is an organ of hearing and equilibrium that detects and analyzes sound by transduction (or converting sound waves into electrochemical impulses) and maintains a sense of balance. For the ear to operate fully, hearing involves the outer, middle, and internal ear and the auditory cortex in the brain. "The external ear helps concentrate the air vibrations on the ear drum and make it vibrate." The vibrations, in turn, are transmitted by a chain of little bones in the middle ear to the inner ear. It is there they arouse the fibers of the auditory nerves to transmit impulses to the brain. Whew, what a multifaceted structure for hearing. As difficult as it is to identify the various sounds we hear daily, comes an even greater complexity involved in deciphering what our students say. Sometimes, we must be astute in our listening so we can hear what they neglect to share. Though it's important to consider what our scholars verbally articulate, listening to non-verbal cues is equally essential. Hearing takes on a different meaning when we are sensitive to deciphering language that is not spoken. Our students say so much. That's why we must hear with our eyes and ears. This sounds like an oxymoronic statement, right? More prevalent than verbal articulation is non-verbal communication. It's the conversation that we see demonstrated by body language. Not only does it speak loudly, but it usually contradicts what our ears hear.

Okay, let me put it in perspective. You heard, "I didn't get a chance to do my homework." But their body language displayed annoyance. Therefore, your response was to the annoyance and not the homework issue. This means we sometimes miss the underlying causes due to the conflict between what we hear versus what is shown. Let me explain. Once, I had a student who acted out three days out of five. Some days I could work through his disruptive behavior. But there were other occasions when I had to call his dad. Initially, he said he came to school to be with his friends. Then there were days when he would sit at the table and refuse to do his work. On one of his good days, he cursed at me, then turned to the sandbox to play with a classmate. Later at circle time, he left the group to go to his cubby and cry. I did not know what to think, and it confused the heck out of me. I had mixed feelings and was at a loss for words for this mixed-blonde, curly-haired three-year-old. Transparent moment, as I looked at his dad's demeanor and the many people that dropped his son off and picked him up from school, I sized him up to be a little thug in the making.

To make a fair assessment of what I saw and heard, I needed to document each occurrence. Unfortunately, what I heard did not mirror what I saw or felt. In fact, I became perplexed about the whole situation. Some days, his actions displayed that he wanted to be in school, yet his words were harsh and uncaring. It was a Monday afternoon when we were transitioning from lunch to rest time when I decided to sit on the floor beside his cot. I rubbed his back with slow, soft, gentle strokes as I sat there. Making small talk, I asked him what he did over the weekend, and I was not ready for his response. This little boy rolled onto his side, looked straight at me, and said, "I hung out with my dad on the corner cause he had to make that paper." Then he rolled back onto his stomach; I was speechless. This time, his words impacted me differently. I heard not only with my ears but also with my heart. Then it dawned on me that my baby was tired when he came to school and was fighting to stay awake and engaged, but it was just too much for him to do. My initial assessment had been all wrong. I could not connect the two because they were contradictory in nature. Now, do you see why it is vital to engage with astuteness to help us when we see one thing but hear something opposing? Using only his skills, he was conveying his inability to stay focused and involved through his inconsistent behavior and emotional outburst. When the day ended, I had to check myself. Meaning I had to look at how I handled that situation and ask myself the hard questions. My first question was, why couldn't I hear his internal cry? Secondly, I wondered why I missed key red flags like disruptive behavior and emotional instability. I had seen this type of behavior before in other students, but I missed it completely with him. Maybe, it was due to my preconceived biases. Nevertheless, children tend to act out when they are tired by becoming overly active and irritable because they are trying to stay awake. To say the least, I was disappointed with myself. No matter how inconsequential we may think the verbal versus non-verbal exchanges are, they are relevant to making informed decisions concerning what we hear.

SCRIPTURE

I hope and pray this makes sense, as we better understand that our ears require incisive translating to hear distinctly. Because we have two ears, it is safe to surmise that we should be more inclined to listen more intently. In fact, they are positioned in such a way they can hear things that are coming from different directions. This is interesting because of what the Bible shares in Mark 4:23-24 (ESV) "If anyone has ears to hear, let him hear." And He said to them, "Pay attention to what you hear: with the measure you use, it will be measured to you, and still more will be added to you." This helped me because it teaches that hearing is more than hearing. It involves listening, which forces us to incorporate the art of disciplining ourselves. More importantly, we must be empathic about how we interpret what we hear because it will have a boomerang effect. In other words, imposing consequences based on a faulty ear will, in turn, come back the same way we send it out. Therefore, when engaging in conversations with our students, we should hear with the goal of understanding so we can properly address any concerns. We also want to deal with infractions lovingly simply because that's how we want to be treated. We might have to wait for our students to share a complete thought before opening our mouths to reply. In other words, we should take the time to process the situation properly, so we don't react. Listening elicits a well-thought-out answer to a situation.

In my early years of teaching, I cannot tell you how often I did not provide an adequate answer to something a student shared with me. First and foremost, I was preoccupied and failed to take the time to stop and listen. As disappointing as this may sound, many of us have been in my shoes, and some still are. To hear the conflicting conversations of your students, you must assess why you hear the way you do and weigh your outlook. Everything points back to the matters of our hearts. There are so many factors responsible for how we differentiate utterances. In this process, we are deciphering the information, gauging it from personal references, and perceiving it as true or not based on what we know or have observed. Without fail, our motive will reveal how we hear and answer, not only with our words but actions. Even now, when I am faced with decisions, I try to make sure I am centered emotionally and mentally. If I fail to do so, my reply will not be constructive, and the aftermath will emerge from a place of emotional baggage. No matter how hard or purposeful we try to be, we are still subject to error. Therefore, the right thing to do is to own up to our mistakes and try to improve the next time. Perfection is not a part of the equation for becoming a great teacher; integrity is.

As we search for ways of continuing to grow, the scripture tells us that the ear of a wise educator pursues knowledge. I don't know about you, but this is a prescription for success. In plain English, when it comes to being alert to the information our students disclose, we must look for insight behind what is not spoken. There are times when our students share concerns that don't make sense. I believe it's because they do not know how to articulate their feelings, or it may be too painful to express. Here is where we stop and lean in. We know what we've heard; now it's time to process what was not disclosed. I'm not trying to beat you over the head; I want us to truly get it. Our role will never be mediocre because of the level of accountability associated with our profession. In the eyes of some students, we personify the love they long to receive. For others, we demonstrate a desire for them to succeed through our patience, guidance, and encouragement. Now, I could be talking from my own biases; however, I have not witnessed any other group of people that embodies as many character traits, gifts, and abilities as we do. We are exceptional! Say it with me, "I am all that!"

Let's Pray:

Father, we ask that you keep us clothed and in our right mind as we do what we believe you have called us to do.
Help us not to get weary in our assignment and take it for granted. We know and accept the responsibility to care for the students you have mandated us to protect, nurture and educate.
Thank you for giving us the strength to endure every twist, turn and trap set for us. We pray for a heart to trust, a mouth to speak the truth in love, eyes to see what is hidden, and ears to hear what is unspoken.
In Jesus' Name, Amen.

RECALIBRATE

There is no turning back; the hard part, in my opinion, you have already done. You are still standing after every setback, lie, and attempt to get you to quit. Though tired, frustrated, and angry at times, your students have consistently been able to pull from your fight and motivation. On that note, you have shown the discipline to become more intentional in hearing the heart of your students. And, because of your desire to refocus your perspective, you hear differently. What they say now has a new meaning than before. Becoming more relational has created an attentiveness that has obligated you to center your thoughts on what matters most. I can feel your apprehension at times, and I am not saying it's not warranted.

However, I want you to remember I've been where you are. So, be confident that you are human and a work in progress. We all are; there are no perfect beings. One thing I know for sure is that you were born for this.

Your constitution dictates that you are not a punk, nor have you ever been. In every situation, you've demonstrated the tenacity to bounce back. There is not one person that can deny your capability to shift the mindset of your students. You've given them reasons to strive for more. Not only that, you have shown them that you are available. As people who have made our mark on society, we have saved many scholars from self-destructing. I am sure a few names and faces come to mind. Hence, jot down those names and reflect on them the next time you feel drained or consider relinquishing your mantle prematurely. I had to remind myself often of my value. But there were other moments when I had to look in the mirror and say, "You are a winner, and your greatest strength lies in your ability to champion your students to the finish line." I want you to affirm this: "All I do is win and will continue to prevail and be an influence on my students."

While you may not share this sentiment, some teach as an occupation, not a passion, a job, not a calling. For us, however, it is a way of life. Instruction is like a second layer of skin, which will remain intact for as long as we are breathing. Accordingly, everywhere I go, I am a teacher; in the grocery store, the park, or just having fun with my grands. During an outing with Jayce, my grandson, a lady watched my interactions with him and asked if I was a teacher. She noticed how I made everything a teachable moment by explaining and giving him the liberty to ask questions. So listen, that's who we are.

Our knack for cultivating is like the commercial Prego, "It's in us!" Today, I challenge you to elevate how you think about what you do. Though we have been given the title of teacher, educator, instructor, mentor, professor, or whatever else people feel like calling us, we supersede these titles because we are multifaceted beings. Trust me! Some days when you walk into your classroom, you can be compared to a physician. Let's consider a few prescriptions you've written for students. Do you remember the students that came to school depressed because of little to no family support? You heard their desperation behind the smiles and laughter each day. You connected them to a team of people who would mentor them in their homework assignments three days a week. What about those barely passing? Your prescription involved building their confidence with a spoken affirmation of their potential. When you look back on the lives you've saved, I am sure you see their faces. Your ability to listen to the subtlest whispers for attention gave you the foresight to tailor each prescription based on the diagnosis.

Never underestimate your superpower, which is your empathic ear, to hear what's being demonstrated by the actions of your students. You will change the game of education when you do. This is not an arrogant statement.

You Are Not Just A Teacher; You Are So Much More!
Darlene Northam

On the contrary, it's true on every level. Even when we get distracted by life and think it is time to do something different, there is a tugging on our hearts. Early on, I talked about encountering a challenging season when I declared I would never step foot in another classroom. The crazy thing was I heard the (wrong) thoughts in my mind and allowed them to convince me to quit. I told my husband I wasn't going back; I was done! I was at home, doing what I equated to mundane daily chores that drove me insane. Of course, this is no shade towards homemakers because they are simply amazing. But something happened. I could not deny nor refute the fire I experienced standing in front of a classroom full of little people, doing what I do best, ensuring they had opportunities to learn. When I interacted with children, no matter their age, I got excited and lit up like a city skyline at night. Mentally and emotionally, I had flashbacks and longed for a fix. I likened my time in the classroom to a healthy addiction. I felt empty and lost without it but alive and free in that setting. Anyone who knew me saw my energy, excitement, laughter, and willingness to inspire. Children fueled me in so many ways. I couldn't stay away. Finally, after eight months of torturing myself, I was presented with an opportunity that gave me hope and a fresh perspective on what it meant to be stretched.

Occasionally, all it takes is a new possibility to realign our focus. This is what working at Head Start did for me. For one thing, it afforded me the privilege of surrounding myself with children who pushed me to expose the deeper content of my heart. And in doing so, I could avail myself in ways I didn't realize I had the capacity for. Meaning I released every part of me to meet the needs of my students. Additionally, I exhausted myself to expand my reach concerning ways to accommodate the challenges of the students in my care. To say the least, the social, mental, and emotional needs were great. When I tell you there were days when I left school completely depleted and drained, believe it! In fact, their situation was different from anything I had encountered before, which shifted my attention from me to them. A great way to stay focused and recall your why is to realize it's not about you. Every reason should point back to the children. The moment we make learning about them, we will hear the direction we are to guide them, which will aid in completing their academic journey.

A lot is riding on your ability to keep your students on the right track. Hearing with intentionality has a significant bearing on the end product. This is connected to our promise when we said yes to the position. I am not sure about you, but for me being able to train my ears to become more thoughtful, not just to sounds but words, was tough. This change pushes us to shift from a head perspective to a matter-of-the-heart viewpoint. In other words, we are given the liberty to hear our students using an ardent ear. Once the adjustment is made, our exchanges with our students will blossom into more meaningful conversations. Keep persisting and moving in the right direction. When necessary, motivate yourself by affirming who you are. Give yourself a pep talk every now and then. You do it for everybody else, so why not for yourself?

RELENTLESS

Consistency is the key. It is the answer to creating successful strategies to keep you focused while pushing forward. I am reminded of the story of the Tortoise and the Hare. Long story short, the story's moral spotlights momentum, not speed. If we are honest with ourselves, some of us have operated like the hare. By this, I mean thinking we could get it all done without considering our emotional and mental needs and, as a result, forgetting to pace ourselves. Though the expectation is the finish line, it should not come at the expense of forsaking our well-being. Without counting the cost, we jet from the starting point, with our eyes fixed on dotting the I's and crossing the T's. I am not suggesting that you are not used to hard work or winning. Obviously, your steadfastness in the past has guided you, which has afforded you some successful outcomes. Unfortunately, this has been your strength and your curse. Hence, you grind, not taking a break when you need to nor ensuring you are emotionally sound enough to forge ahead. After an intense lead, your body slows down, and you begin to experience fatigue. Thinking you have time to finish everything on your plate, you stop. No, you crash. When you come to yourself, you realize that you are burnt out.

You Are Not Just A Teacher; You Are So Much More!
Darlene Northam

We cannot always live up to the expectations of others, sometimes, not even our own. Nevertheless, take the necessary steps to hear what your body is saying and prepare to slow down. Don't rush the process by allowing the sound of trouble and dismay to cause you to miss critical moments. Your students are counting on you to model the actions of the tortoise by assessing every possibility and opportunity because they need you to finish strong. For this cause, we should consider our obligation as privileged. There is much work to do; children will experience loss without you in the classroom. The necessity of it all is found in our ability to sustain our attention and not allow the pressures of our environment to cause us to stop running. We must learn to build up a speed that we can maintain. In some cases, speed is essential, but not without our capacity to make consistent and intentional strides to accomplish our objective. Know that the winner of a race is not always the fastest out the gate but the teacher who is persistent in displaying the temperament to complete the task effectively. Get your mojo back and find a rhythm that suits your running style. A few more laps, and you will be there. The greatest part about this victory is hearing your students cheering you on.

LISTEN!

I've come to recognize that the more successful instructors can readily adapt to their setting by making every part of themselves available to their students. Our scholars need the flexibility to access all of us. When we come to school, we should be physically, socially, mentally, and emotionally present. Our pupils must know they are important to us, which can only be demonstrated by how we respond. During conversations, we must practice active listening. Defined, "active listening is a way of listening and responding to another person that improves mutual understanding." Though we may have a million other things to do, we cannot allow ourselves to become distracted to the point we ignore them. It is easy to become preoccupied with things that always need our attention. However, when we wear our teacher's hat, nothing, and I do mean nothing, is more important than they are. There is zilch that can replace the feeling of a student returning to say, "Thank You!" Be the best you, every day, and I guarantee you that the memories you carry throughout your journey will reignite the fire that burns within.

5

The Hands of a Teacher

"It is in your hands to create a better world for all who live in it."
Nelson Mandela

Louis Nizer says this about hands, "A man who works with his hands is a laborer; a man who works with hands and his brain is a craftsman; but a man who works with his hands, brain, and heart is an artist." Now, that speaks to who we are in a nutshell. We are professionals that have been tasked with creating one-of-a-kind masterpieces. Our students are on the potter's wheel. Our hands remain in constant contact as we mold and shape them into successful and skillful individuals. In one quote, Nizer describes the completeness of educators. And once again, solidifies the value of establishing harmony between our hearts and intelligence. We are not whole without that alignment. Our role is all-inclusive; everything a child will need is wrapped in our bundle package. We possess the gifts that keep giving: our hearts, mouths, eyes, ears, and hands. Unfortunately, we cannot pick which part of us will not be available on any given day. That's just not feasible. It's all or nothing. As I share what it means to be more of a total package, I pray that I've demonstrated in very practical ways how life-altering it is for students to interact with teachers who see the relevance in making every part of themselves accessible.

With that being said, how do we engage our hands in mentoring our students, thereby impacting their lives? For starters, we need to understand what our hands do and how they are associated with other parts of our anatomy. According to Merriam-Webster's definition of the hand, "They are a terminal part of the vertebrate forelimb when modified (as in humans) as a grasping organ: the body part at the end of the arm of a human, ape, or monkey." In addition to knowing what the hands are, we must comprehend their function. As documented in an online writeup by physio-pedia.com, the chief function of our hands is to be able to manipulate objects that accomplish an objective. "The ability of a human hand to assure a myriad of positions and to apply only the precise amount of pressure necessary to hold an object is due to the mobility and stability supplied by the skeleton, the power of the muscle, the remarkable degree of sensory feedback from the nerves."

I like the medical definition; however, I want to share a few more thoughts concerning the function of our hands. With our hands, we interact with our students on so many levels. For instance, with younger students, we assist them with their fine-motor skills and occasionally getting in or out of a coat or jacket. If you have worked as a Head Start teacher, you may have been responsible for showing students how to use utensils, feed themselves, and brush their teeth. Our hands also offer a soft touch to a child needing comfort or reassurance. As one who spent a great majority of time working with younger children, my hands have been known to rub the backs of little ones as they fall to sleep. Though our hands have multiple uses, we never want to be found guilty of using them to harm a student.

Over my lifetime, I have witnessed teachers escorted out of the building because their hands were used inappropriately. Hitting, smacking, pushing, grabbing, or shoving a pupil is unacceptable. I do not care how upset we may become. Go home, quit if that will save a child from a traumatic experience; spare your reputation and possibly jail time. At any rate, our hands are essential, and we must utilize them in beneficial ways.

In contrast, what happens when we do not have the full capability and use of our hands? Okay, let me ask it this way. What takes place in the life of an instructor who has limited use of his appendages? Most would consider it a handicap. Merriam-Webster defines handicap as a disadvantage that makes achievement usually difficult. The hindrance does not make the task impossible, just challenging. How, then, is one able to accomplish the necessary day-to-day expectations? This is a very relevant question because touching the lives of our mentees does not always constitute a physical connection.

From my experience, something more effective than a bodily touch is having an astute awareness to reach a student emotionally. Working with children who have suffered trauma, a physical hands-on approach may not always be the best way to connect with that student. In other words, that child may not be receptive to a hand touch because it may serve as a trigger. For this reason, we must elicit aid from our perceptive nature to meet those needs. I dare not say that sometimes before we are in a position to satisfy the academic struggles of our kids, we must break through emotional barriers. Nothing will be impossible once we have aligned with their heart, and they know we can be trusted. I have experienced guards coming down and students welcoming the opportunity to learn.

Let me tell you a quick yet relevant story. During year fifteen, I encountered a little boy who was not feeling me, his classmates, or anything that resembled school. He had separation anxiety and was emotionally detached. When I stooped to place my arms around his small frame, he never looked at me, nor did his arms reciprocate my attempted warm embrace. He just stood there with his head in the lock of his shoulder, staring at the floor. At that point, I knew my work was cut out for me. After the first day, he would have meltdowns and throw tantrums during circle time. Some days he didn't nap; if he did, it took about thirty minutes for him to wind down and drift off to sleep. For about a month and a half, I sought ways to reach this student because he was not participating in classroom activities. Most days, he would stay to himself and watch the other children. I needed divine intervention. So, one day I asked God for some wisdom that would allow this child to open up to me. I wanted him to know that I could see his frustration. I could hear his cries for attention though he never opened his mouth. I didn't want to necessarily touch him physically; I just needed to reach where he was hurting the most. That place was not visible, which required me to be creative in my planning.

After many attempts, I finally believed I had a strategy that would work. I began to utilize the thirty minutes it took him to wind down for naptime as some one-on-one time. I had to ease him into it, but slowly he caught on. I created a learning station of fun and games. He thought we were playing, but you all know I was assessing skills while building a relationship. This little boy pulled on so many of my emotions. To look at him, no one would recognize how much protentional had been locked up inside. Maybe, buried is a better word. He isolated himself because he felt safe in that space. Until this point, he refused to allow anyone into his bubble. All that changed the day he permitted me to enter his world. For once in his young life, I believe he recognized someone's ability to acknowledge him for who he was. And, in doing so, I was allowed to touch him in a way not even his mom had been able to. Trust was the foundation for establishing our union and helping me get to where he could begin his academic journey. He became one of my best scholars. The day I administered the Phonological Awareness Literacy Screening (PALS) to him, I cried because of how well he did.

Remain open to the various ways to touch our students; remember, it's not always the physical interaction that reaches them. I say this because our first attempt should be to meet them where they are. We cannot get them where they need to be if we don't start at the beginning. It's much like walking somewhere. If we take them by the hand and walk side-by-side, we will get them to cross the finish line. Securing their hand with an intentional embrace creates a meshing of our hearts. Undoubtedly, we must put in the work by any means necessary to get it done. Of course, I am not suggesting that you haven't. All I want you to do right now is take a minute and reflect on all of the hearts you've touched as a result of the hands you've held.

SCRIPTURE

Yes, connecting with your students through touch is essential and can change the trajectory of their lives. Moreover, the magnitude of it will surpass our lifetime because of the domino effect it will have on generations to come. Whether we impact students with the sensitivity of our hearts or words, they will continue to evolve. Our influence will prevail for some because of our aptitude to see and engage with them. Even more important will be our skillset to discern the meaning behind unspoken words. With all of the responsibility of being a teacher, let's not assume that our guidance, understanding, and longevity have anything to do with our strength. If we are honest, we will acknowledge that there is a power and presence that has guided us through our journey. In fact, the hand of God has been present every step of the way, as evident by our still standing. We cannot do what we do in our own might. Just as our hands are used to alter the lives of our mentees, so are the hands of Jesus, as stated in the text below.

Matthew 19:13,15 says this about the significance of hands. "One day, some parents brought their children to Jesus so he could lay his hands on them and pray for them. But the disciples (those men that hung out with Jesus) scolded the parents for bothering him. And he placed his hands on their heads and blessed them before he left" (NLT). I became somewhat upset when I observed how disconnected the disciples were in their relationship with Jesus. They had walked closely with him and still did not know his heart concerning children, so he reprimanded them. More than anyone else, they should have known. These two scripture verses speak volumes concerning how Jesus viewed the little ones. This example of Jesus' physical touch reminds us that we, too, must identify moments when a touch is warranted. Nothing is more gratifying than seeing a child gain the confidence to finish a difficult task because of a reassuring encounter. Sometimes, all it takes is a gentle hand touch resting on a shoulder or connecting hand to hand that sends the most powerful messages. Their premise for bringing them to Jesus was two-folded, prayer and blessings. Children are our foundation. And, if we get it right at the rudimentary level, what a great start we'll have to build upon. I know this is one of the reasons I was convicted not to leave the younger age groups.

Yes, I have a story for you. You knew one was coming. It was during my third year of teaching at a Christian Academy. A couple of teachers began to stroke my ego by telling me how wonderful and gifted I was. They suggested I go to our principal and request a move to a higher-grade level. I entertained the thought for a little during that afternoon. Later that day, as I packed my things to go home, it was as if God came and stood in my classroom. All I heard was, "I wish you would ask your boss permission to change your assignment. I placed you where you are, not her. I can't trust everyone with my little ones. They need special people who will always remember what it was like being a child. You touch them in such a way they are not intimidated to be themselves." I was speechless. Everything I had in my hands hit the floor; I mean everything. All I could do was cry and ask for forgiveness. Yes, I cry often, and my friends tease me about it. I felt ashamed, to say the least. God trusted me, and I could not see it. After I regained my composure, I wiped my tears, held my head up, and walked my hips out of the door. After that, it was clear where I belonged, and I never thought about leaving pre-k until I was certain it was time to do

You Are Not Just A Teacher; You Are So Much More!
Darlene Northam

something different. I was scared straight that day. I did some remediation with middle schoolers for a principal I had a relationship with but nothing permanent.

If it was relevant for Jesus to physically touch children, how essential is it for us to do the same? Not only is it necessary in a tangible sense but also in a way that addresses various needs. I guarantee you will encounter students requiring some form of connection with you. However, some may not articulate what they want to say because they may not know how. In that regard, you must observe their actions to activate your perception. Your capacity to be vulnerable and know how to reach your mentees will be crucial as you learn who they are and what each one may need. In fact, establishing purposeful relations with your students will create meaningful bonds that will blossom into blessings for each of you.

Say this prayer with me.

Father, thank you for allowing me to steward your children. Help me not to discount my obligation to those you have placed in my care. Give me the wisdom, knowledge, and understanding required to train them for a world that may not be ready for them or welcome them with open arms. Give them the strength and fortitude to be true to whom you have called them to be and give me the boldness to speak words that inspire and challenge them to be great.
In Jesus' Name, Amen.

RECALIBRATE

Thank you for praying with me. Listen, desiring to maintain relevance in your pupils' lives will continue growing as you stay engaged. Now that your outlook has changed relish your hand's power to motivate and empower. You have great influence, and with it comes hope and limitless possibilities. Therefore, I encourage you not to shrink back into stagnancy but rather utilize every opportunity to point your students in the right direction. As moments present themselves, use your hands to communicate in ways you haven't done before. Some days you may find it necessary to place your hand gently on your student's shoulder to reassure them. Think shift, and you will always seek fresh and new avenues.

You are ready to soar with the eagles as you make the essential strides to break through barriers that once held you captive. You transform lives once your mind becomes free from stigmas or outdated thought processes. Keep in mind that daily connections must be made with your scholars. Learning to touch them as individuals is imperative because one variation could make the difference in keeping them engaged or losing them altogether. As you continue to alter how you use your hands, explore new ideas that will cause your students to see you more meaningfully. And in doing so, you will acquire greater creativity, yielding unique outcomes. For example, learning to unite or reconnect with your pupils may mean revamping your class schedule to set aside time for heart-to-heart chats. This modification will touch a place in their emotional space and allow them to feel the warmth of your planned closeness. Think about it this way; when we lean in to listen to someone speaking, it sends the message that we are interested. There's no better way to gain trust and establish secure relationships.

This meaningful deviation will speak volumes, and teaching will become less laboring because of a different approach. Undoubtedly, this will leave a more intimate impression. Hence, they will recognize and appreciate your eagerness to keep plugging. Assuredly, it is important to remain flexible to maintain a consistent presence, which is the only way to continue to evolve. Another means of recalibrating would be to become interested in things they like and enjoy doing. It is praiseworthy to make a slight adjustment. You may not witness it right away; however, eventually, you will begin to see the gratitude from students.

For the record, our hands serve as multipurpose appendages, as they can make a lasting impression without making human contact. This reminds me of how purposeful sign language is and the strength that is demonstrated in the art of verbal exchanges. There are so many hand gestures, symbols, and signs you can implement to reach the heart of your students. So, as you become more determined to change what was once familiar, push yourself to always look for occasions to force yourself out of complacency. Your hands will become a great asset if you revere them as a source of persuasion.

You Are Not Just A Teacher; You Are So Much More!
Darlene Northam

From the word go, you jumped into the classroom with both feet planted firmly, not half-stepping but learning as you progress. With all you have acquired, you are ready for this last shove. Remain focused, faithful, and finish strong. Don't allow the small or large bumps in the road to throw you too far out of alignment. Pull over and get your second wind when necessary because I am clapping loudly for you.

RELENTLESS

Without the assistance of your hands, I don't know how much you would accomplish. They have provided you with the ability to comfort, reinforce, encourage, and guide. It's not what you say but how you say it; sometimes, a gentle touch can say it best. Working with young minds often requires lots of connectivity. They need that security, which gives them the confidence to achieve. So, from now on, when you walk into your classroom, please don't neglect your hands, as they are an essential part of your teaching.

Take note, not only are our hands vital for the emotional stability of our students, but also their physical aspect. Our hands do the work that our hearts tell them to. For example, our empathy tells the hands to wipe the tears from the eyes of a fallen child. Our hands will also aid in writing narratives of the lives we have influenced throughout our pilgrimage. In addition, we need them to document our story long after we have left the classroom. So, take care of your hands and nurture them with the utmost care.

You Are Not Just A Teacher; You Are So Much More!
Darlene Northam

I am one of your biggest fans and committed advocates because I am acquainted with the struggle. Over the past two years, I have gained a deeper appreciation for teachers. I say this because of your tenacity and ability to endure Covid19 and still operate with compassion and grace. Simply put, you have opened my eyes to a different breed of educator. The DNA you possess has surpassed that of instructors in my day and those that have taken the stance that teaching is just something to do. I can only imagine your drive, among other things, the thoughts that keep you girded with the determination to forge ahead. As you anticipate the path in front of you, fix your eyes on the future lives you are destined to impact. Allow your hands to assist you in clearing the way and pushing past obstacles designed to slow you down. Not only will your hands be used to support you, but also that of your mentees. Many of them will gain strength because of your emotional association. The thought of their teacher affirming their efforts and accomplishments will paint a positive picture of who you have become. You are in the classroom with these scholars and see their challenges. What better way to help them change their story than through the praise of your handclap? Celebrate them as often as it takes. Though doing this for your students is necessary, it is equally important for you. Pat yourself on the back and say, "I am amazing!" Don't be dismayed if it takes you more than once to believe it; say it as many times as it takes to grasp the thought. Other ways to keep you stepping in the right direction may include giving yourself a high-five and slapping your hand. You don't have to wait for anyone else to do it because only you know what is required to pick you up and get you going.

Your hands are essential in reconfiguring the way lessons should be taught. Hence, you can mold and shape them to reinforce whatever you teach. Because of your ability to make memorable connections with your class, your existence is felt even when you are not around. Your authority touches and reminds them of the life lessons you have shared, which they hold dear. But it's more than your physical prod that stimulates them to prepare academically and for life beyond school. Consider the magnitude of your artwork. You have created masterpieces that you can now put on display. You have molded and fashioned students who were lifeless and withdrawn into priceless one-of-a-kind individuals. These students have silently watched you maneuver through rough patches in the road. Though pissed off some days, you never relinquished your responsibility to ensure their success. Because of your hands-on approach, you have shown how vital it is for them to endure.

POWERFUL HANDS

John R. W. Stott says, "Leaders have power, but the power is safe only in the grasp of those who humble themselves to serve." To make this assertion concerning your hands, I know you have put yourself in the trenches with your students and work. Subsequently, you have demonstrated resilience in your efforts to lead by example. As educators, we have been commissioned to steward the minds of those in our sphere of authority. As those with rule, we must not misuse our platform to manipulate or exploit our scholars. Let me say this: emphatic hands know how to rebuke and redirect simultaneously. However, I want to point out that the power resides in how the correction is done. Students respond differently when they know your intent is noble. With this in mind, I want to quote a line from the movie Spider-Man. "With great power comes great responsibility." We are called to offer a helping hand, not conditionally but unconditionally.

In conclusion, I want you to revere your impact on imparting knowledge that you have at your fingertips. Powerful hands know when to relate and release for the purpose of preparing students. In addition, hands are astutely aware of the need to build up and restore. As people who have changed many narratives, let us continue to be that source of strength that will always be critical in pointing others in the direction they should go. With one hand signal, Malcolm X released a hand gesture that mobilized an army of Islamic men to stand their ground. During a "Black Lives Matter" protest, a closed hand formed a clenched fist that signified resiliency and the power to keep going despite the struggle. Educators, we have touched lives from infancy to adulthood. With each touch, we have shaped every student that has crossed our doorsill, so

You Are Not Just A Teacher; You Are So Much More!
Darlene Northam

let's celebrate this accomplishment. Remember, it's how we use our hands that makes them powerful.

6

The Arms of a Teacher

"Opening his arms, he said quietly to her, "Disappear here."
—*Jonathan Carroll*

I assumed I was finished with this book. However, it wasn't until my book coach and publisher, Monique Jewell Anderson, suggested that I highlight two essential limbs. I cannot say I was thrilled because I was not. For a brief minute or so, I had some choice words brewing under my breath but quickly regained my composure because it wasn't personal. In fact, her role during this process was to challenge me; to put on paper those things that were in my heart, not just for me but also for you. Nevertheless, as I pondered what I would write, I reflected on my first book draft and its title. The irony is that my first manuscript was entitled "The Power of A Hug." So, it's only befitting that I conclude with a chapter on arms.

Throughout my teaching career, I took pride that my arms were a secret weapon. In fact, I was known for my transformative hugs. Hence, they stopped tears from crying students and soothed the hearts of moms leaving their child(ren) in a new environment for the first time. My warm embraces reassured me and filled spaces where doubt and anxiety once were. For that student who didn't feel loved or appreciated, hugs served as validation and a safe place. In addition, my arms sometimes provided the confidence and the tenacity to press past opposition and barriers designed to keep students from achieving academic success.

Let me just say this, as educators, you, too, have this weapon in your arsenal. Use it to your advantage. Not only will you see a difference in your student's behavior, but you will also win parents' approval. With this in mind, never underestimate its ability to create a nurturing classroom atmosphere. Though the classroom culture has changed, physical hugs may not be permissible in some institutions, but they are essential. Therefore, I encourage you to always search for ways to provide that desired sense of comfort and reassurance that all students need at some point in their journey.

Just as vital as hugs are for our students, they are even more advantageous for us. Why would I say this? Well, I liken it to self-care. We are better positioned to care for others when we attend to our needs. In other words, we become empty if we always give and pour ourselves into others. Learning how to extend that same level of care and concern to ourselves will also transform our lives on every level possible. I had to learn this principle through trial and error. Believe it or not, research shows the therapeutic gains of hugs and how they can alter our physical and emotional state.

I recently listened to a recent online article entitled, 6 Amazing Benefits of Hugs You Never Knew About, which gives credence to the fact that we need more of them. After reading about the health rewards of extending warm embraces, I immediately thought about your work environment and how cool it would be to have hugs daily. You would probably be surprised at the number of people who don't receive them. Can you imagine the type of atmosphere that would create? Once again, I realize people have become hesitant about close contact since the pandemic. So, I leave it up to your discretion. However, as human beings, we have an innate longing to give and receive affection. It starts the moment we exit the womb. Nurturing is the sustaining force required for babies to develop properly through the stages of life and is absolutely vital.

According to the article, hugs improve self-esteem because of the security and confidence it provides through touch. Secondly, it is an alternative to communicating with someone; it's non-verbal. Thirdly, it reduces our level of stress and anxiety. Wow! Is this not powerful? Hugging has a calming effect. Think about how often you have stopped or reduced the level of intensity of a student having a meltdown. You may have employed other methods, but they foiled. However, as soon as you wrapped your arms around that student, it was as if the waterworks stopped, utter silence. With the stress of being an educator, we can benefit from having a healthier heart. The article states that "hugs are part of a physical manifestation of love. In fact, when we embrace someone, oxytocin is increased, a powerful neurotransmitter that provides pleasure and reduces physical and mental discomfort. In all of that, it supports our cardiovascular system and heart."

And lastly, they increase serotonin levels, according to Elena Martinez Blasco, the writer. "Serotonin is a chemical that our body secretes and acts as a neurotransmitter. When we embrace someone, we increase those levels and feel pleasure and happiness." I need a hug, do you? Of course, you do. Due to the complexity of our careers, we need as many embraces as it takes to keep our focus and grounded.

As I close, please pray this prayer with me.

Father, thank you for allowing me to use my arms as a source of comfort when caring for your children.
Thank you for reminding me that I am an instrument of your love and kindness to those I am called to serve.
When students need encouragement, gentle reminders of who they are, or just a tender touch, help me remember that there is transforming power in a hug. Thank you for the ability to discern when they can benefit from a warm embrace.
In Jesus Name. Amen.

7

The Final Words for Teachers

Listen, my whole premise for writing this book and inviting you to take this journey with me was to remind you of who you are and the power each of you possesses as those who lay the foundation for so many people. But, more importantly, I wanted you to see yourself as I see you, a whole being who cannot afford to mismanage opportunities of changing students' lives. So, every day you walk into your place of influence, remember to take your heart, mouth, eyes, ears, hands, and arms with you. They are essential in accomplishing the task before you. Each student will require something different, so use every resource in your toolbelt because you will need it.

I applaud your efforts for continuing to improve and perform at unparalleled excellence. Your students' lives will forever be impacted, not only because of what you do but because of how you do it. Your fortitude, laced with patience and love, has been your badge of honor, and you have worn it proudly. So, with my arms wide open and my heart filled with love and gratitude, please allow me to wrap my arms around you and give you one of my most transforming hugs. You deserve

You Are Not Just A Teacher; You Are So Much More!
Darlene Northam

it! You guys make me grateful to stand tall among an elite force because *You Are Not Just A Teacher; You Are So Much More!*

About the Author

Darlene Northam, a native of Portsmouth, VA, received her early education in the Portsmouth Public School system. She graduated from Woodrow Wilson High School and continued her love of learning by attending Tidewater Community College. There she received associate degrees in early childhood and education/general Studies.

Darlene's thirst for knowledge drew her to Norfolk State University, where she earned a bachelor's degree in interdisciplinary studies and a Master's in Pre-Elementary Education.

As an educator for over twenty-two plus years, Darlene has utilized her passion for transforming the lives of young people by serving them in various institutional settings. She has worked with third and fourth graders as a SOL remediation tutor in Math. In addition, Darlene has taught students in the private Christian school setting, daycare, and Head Start. She also held the position of principal in her desire to impact more lives than those in the classroom. As well, Darlene has held positions as an afterschool and daycare director. Darlene has taught not only in Virginia but also in the state of South Carolina.

Darlene is proud of her accomplishments as a mentor and 2010 Teacher of The Year. Her most recent achievement is that of author for her book, You Are Not Just A Teacher; You Are So Much More! With all that Darlene has achieved, she is a down-to-earth, personable, transparent individual who loves people. Her affection for seeing educators thrive and become all God has purposed for them is always at the forefront of her heart. As a means of helping them accomplish this, Darlene provides professional development, motivational speeches, and training. She also does workshops, teacher retreats and offers individualized teacher mentorship.

You can connect with the educator-midwife and author, at darlenenortham7@gmail.com, and social media platforms, and at www.darlenenortham.com.

Darlene Northam, Pre-Elementary, ED., M.A.
Educator, Motivational Speaker, Author

You Are Not Just A Teacher; You Are So Much More!
Darlene Northam

Works-cited

Chapter 2
Online article, How the pandemic has changed teachers' commitment to remaining in the classroom www.brookings.com
(www.dictionary.cambridge.org)

Chapter 3
(www.Medicinenet.com & www.kidhealth.org)

Chapter 4
The Human Eye-Structure and Functioning byjus.com
www.https://byjus.com/physics/structure-human-eye-functioning

Chapter 5
https://www.usip.org/public-education-new/what-active-listening
(Britannica.com)

Chapter 6
www.physio-pedia.com/Hand_Function

Chapter 7
SteptoHealth.com,
www.merriam-webster.com

www.ingramcontent.com/pod-product-compliance
Lightning Source LLC
Chambersburg PA
CBHW071249070526
44583CB00017B/2386